SETTLE IT!

A Self-Help Guide for
SOLVING YOUR CONFLICTS

Illustrated by LAM QUACH

KARIN VAGISTE

STERLING HOUSE
New York ● Toronto ● Stockholm

Canadian Cataloguing in Publication Data
Karin Vagiste
SETTLE IT! : a self-help guide for solving your conflicts

Includes bibliographical references.
ISBN 0-9682157-1-8

1. Conflict Management.   2. Mediation.   1. Title

BF637.M4V34 1999   303.6'9   C99-900998-2

Photography, Joe Lavee, Taylor Hudson
Text Design and Layout, Robert Shmayda
Cover Design, John Melnick & Tannice Goddard

Printed in Canada by Transcontinental Printing

Dedicated to CJ with love.
Thank-you for your joyful
celebration of life.

Acknowledgments

It's been a highlight of my life to have worked with so many fine people who devoted their talents to this book without expecting *anything* in return. Their steadfast belief in the value of this book encouraged me to carry on to completion. I thank them for their unwavering dedication.

Lam Quach completed all the illustrations in far more depth and detail than I dreamed was possible. Robert Shmayda, my computer course instructor, created my page layout and design with fine artistry. A very special thanks to Isabel Molino and Corey Singer for permitting me to photograph them over and over again, for the front cover. John Melnick, my daughter's soccer coach, put all the elements of the cover together with great verve and panache. Tannice Goddard added her vision to the final look of the cover.

I was honored to have several mediators review my manuscript. Cliff Hendler, an insurance dispute mediator and Joan Sinclair who practices family mediation, which is at the other end of the mediation spectrum, provided me with valuable insights. Other reviewers included Solange De Santis, Sean Pigott, Peter Bruer, Nadine Armstrong, Bruce Ally and Dania Lebovics. I was fortunate to hear the candid evalutions of all those who attended the focus groups for the book's cover.

My editors, David McCabe and Susan McNish, went well above the call of duty. Judi Lee-Mckee and Carolyn Wood are great leaders in their respective fields of printing and distribution. They taught me so much.

I express my gratitude to my daughter, who put up with the piles and piles of rewrites. Thanks for wading through the papers to give me your supportive hugs. I'm glad you participated as my co-author.

I thank each person for collaborating in the true spirit of mediation as we problem-solved together. I extend my deepest appreciation to you all.

Contents

A PERSONAL PREFACE

I was having a difficult time rewriting the ninth version of my manuscript for this book, when a man rolled into my life and eased my pain, quite by accident. He was a tow truck driver who had come to pickup my car after my engine coolant had leaked out. It's not what he did, it's what he *said* that rescued me from my mental fatigue. He reminded me why I was writing this book, from a fresh, new perspective.

He was a talkative, high-energy guy who complained about all the overtime he'd been given by his boss. I asked if he had young children waiting for him at home. He sighed his relief saying it was good that he and Lynn didn't have any kids because he just moved out on her two weeks ago. He couldn't stand all the fighting that had gone on every single day. They'd fight about things that weren't even important to either one of them. In a quieter, reflective voice he said that he had really loved her, but all the fighting had worn out his love. I gently explored his predicament a little bit further by asking him to think back to the last big conflict he had had with her. If that conflict had been solved successfully, I asked, did he think all their subsequent fighting would have built up to such a fever pitch? He said probably not. I expressed how sad it is that the unfinished business of one conflict spills over into the next conflict, and the one after that and so on. We sat there quietly reflecting on that sobering thought.

I returned to my computer to complete my manuscript with renewed enthusiasm. Life is too short to spend time on fighting! We spin through our daily routines so quickly that we aren't able to make a sincere effort to solve the many different conflicts that come our way. People usually resort to fighting for

these three reasons:
1. a lack of time to sit down and talk without interruptions for at least fifty minutes;
2. a lack of knowledge about alternative methods for solving a conflict;
3. a lack of self control; our instinct to fight is stronger than our will to make peace.

The comedian, Michael J. Fox said, "Let's do what the typical American family does in the face of a conflict. Sweep it under a rug, get drunk and forget about it."

Conflict doesn't have to be a bad experience. In fact, something good can result from your conflict when you move it through The Action Plan which is described in this book. This Plan is a practical, six step conflict resolution process that uses mediation strategies. We all need a variety of strategies with which to solve the conflicts that inevitably emerge at home, school or work. School and work based peer mediators can use the questions listed in chapter six as their actual script during the mediation meeting. A parent can take on the role of a mediator and solve a dispute between two children. That same parent can follow The Action Plan and also solve a conflict that he himself may have with his employer, neighbor, spouse or a construction worker he has hired. DO-IT-YOURSELF MEDIATION steps are embedded in The Action Plan. It all boils down to the same conflict resolution process. There is a marvelous flexibility built into this process, so that it can address a surprisingly wide range of disputes.

You can improve your chances for a promotion at work when you *use* conflict resolution skills. A typical job interview today will include questions about how the applicant solves conflicts. These skills are a basic requirement for success. Anyone can achieve a more harmonious life by using conflict resolution skills to solve current disputes, as well as disputes that have gone on for years. If you plan to hire a mediator, this book will prepare you for a successful mediation experience.

How far will you allow your anger over an unresolved

conflict to escalate, before you take action? When you read about the Science of Anger you will understand whether your anger is controlling you or you are controlling it. It has been said that you can measure the size of a person by what makes him or her angry.

I believe the anger in our world has been heating up for a long time, but most of us aren't aware of it. This 'heating-up' process is similar to what a person I'll call Jackie, experiences when she's taking a bath. She's been in the bathtub for quite a while reading a book. During that time she's been making the water hotter and hotter. Jackie has no idea how hot the water has become until John enters the bathroom and dips his toe in. He howls in pain because the water has burned his skin. Jackie expresses her genuine surprise, because to her the water isn't that hot. Her comfort level has numbed her to the pain.

I observe people who have become numb to the rude and angry behavior of their family and friends. Over the years they have become more and more comfortable with words and actions that used to cause hurt feelings. Many adults tolerate the disrespect young people shove in their faces, and corporate warfare has become a common, dirty game played by the in-crowd.

Unfortunately, not much happens until the level of anger has heated up to an intense level. Anger went past that point and exploded in a Colorado high school in 1999, when teenagers murdered other teens. There was a message in those murders. Everyone's voice needs to be heard. We can't afford to ignore the expression of anger in the initial stages of a dispute. If we are numb to an early call for help, the anger will build till someone is forced to act. Why wait for an emergency?

The teen murderers didn't fit into that Colorado school culture that glorified the macho athlete. On *48 HRS* students from that high school reported that teachers did nothing when they heard the derogatory and humiliating language that was hurled at the outsiders. They didn't count. They didn't have a voice. Without a voice they lacked power, so the gun became their final,

11

desperate voice. Their gunshots echoed across the world and soon everyone was talking about them. They had finally been heard.

The Colorado students pursued a **destructive expression of anger** because they believed there was no alternative available to them. If the first few conflicts between the in-crowd and the outsiders had been resolved, even partially resolved, there could have been some degree of closure. Their anger would not have exploded in such a tragic manner. But their voices were not heard. They believed that no one cared, so why should they care?

Working as a mediator, I've come to realize that alternative dispute resolution is the best kept secret around. The word has not yet leaked out that this style of solving conflicts is a healthy, **constructive outlet for anger**. It is relevant to the fights between the school boys in blue jeans as well as the business 'boys' in blue suits. (The word boys could be replaced by men, girls or women.) Mediation is the alternative method of resolving conflicts in *any situation* where there's a clash of needs and interests. Of course when someone is pointing a gun at you, you don't hang around to mediate. I have simplified the mediation strategies that I use, so that they can be put to into practice immediately via The Action Plan.

My goal is to turn mediation into a popular activity! The Action Plan includes some exercises that will make you laugh if you decide to try them out. In sharing some laughter with your 'opponent' the tension between you is reduced considerably.

I encourage parents to use mediation in the home in order to reinforce what their children are learning at school. The easiest way to maintain a harmonious home atmosphere is by beginning conflict resolution when your children are young. Of-course don't leave your partner out of it. It is ideal to begin practicing those skills with your partner *before* your children arrive! The vast majority of North American schools have conflict resolution built into the curriculum. If you child's school isn't teaching it then request it. May we begin to apply first aid to the broken hearts of fighters, in the same that way we apply first aid to broken bones. If the heart has been healed, then the hand won't form a tight fist.

A fight, be it verbal or physical, has never solved a dispute. A fight just leads to a revenge attack in some way or other. The tension keeps building till it reaches the unbearable point that my tow truck driver experienced. Eventually he had to run away from the war zone in order to save his sanity.

The 21st Century will see a celebration of multiple alternatives, such as alternative medicine, alternative investing, right along with alternative dispute resolution. The attractive feature that they share is this; they all address the deep desire people have for taking control of their lives.

In alternative medicine, you decide whether to fulfill a doctor's prescription or select a homeopathic remedy. In alternative investing, you can go on-line and make your own investment decisions, thus rejecting a broker's choices. In alternative dispute resolution you are in charge of defining the terms of your resolution. If the dispute is headed toward court, you may not trust a judge to come up with a *fair* decision. Even if your dispute is not headed toward court, conflict resolution will enable you to reach a satisfactory outcome. The fighting that at times seemed endless, will finally be over.

The Action Plan is at the very heart of my book because it represents a new way of getting along with others. It fulfills our basic human need for respect and dignity in the resolution of difficult disputes. Best of all, you will be able to make the important decisions in your life through collaboration. This leads to a strong sense of personally owning your solution which accounts for the high success rate of mediated conflicts. In the words of Dr. Cherie Carter-Scott, "You don't need outside experts, including friendly advice. All your answers lie inside you."[1] If you own the conflict, then the best solution to it lies within you. This book will guide you to it.

Live out your dreams in the 21st Century, by **taking charge** of how you solve the disputes that block you from achieving your goals.

FOREWORD
REVISED AS
FOREPICTURE

Here is a visual summary of THE ACTION
PLAN, which is described in chapters 1, 5 & 6.

Chapter One

Unfinished business doesn't go away. It keeps repeating itself, until it gets our attention, until we feel it, deal with it, and heal.

Melody Beattie

Getting Started

Are you tired of fighting? Have you been through one too many battles that didn't get solved? If you're just warming up for another feisty round of your heated quarrel,...

...then take a detour and travel down a different road. I have carefully mapped out a new way of solving conflicts. We all desire good, solid solutions, because they can rebuild relationships that have gone bad. Lengthy ongoing disputes rob us of vital energy, making us feel stressed-out and therefore worn-out. So even if you've had some sleepless nights, there's no need to age prematurely!

The journey ahead will rejuvenate you by providing a fresh perspective on your old dispute. Such a perspective will open a new window in your world through which you can reach a satisfying solution. We all enjoy experiencing novel worlds of amazing possibilities! That's why people venture forth on a trip in the first place – to touch the incredible Norwegian Fjords, or to feel the thrill of an African Safari! I'll help you to reach out and touch your dream – you *can* achieve the solution that is now only in your fantasy, or your second back-up fantasy, otherwise known as Plan B!

Most people begin a trip knowing where it will end. Wouldn't it be great to have the key that will unlock the door at your destination, *before* you even start your trip? It's my pleasure to hand over a special key that will unlock the solution to your conflict. Thus upon your arrival, you'll be able to relax because your dispute has been cleared away.

WELCOME ABOARD!

As your guide, I'll lead you through your 'internal' landscape. We will visit some sultry and, at times, scorching regions where red-hot anger has created valleys of deep-seated hatred and hostility. We will untangle the tightly knotted undergrowth of disappointment that has been created by the dispute.

If you feel the least bit anxious about taking your first few steps, then the words of Albert Einstein will provide you with comfort and encouragement. He tells us WHY we are on this journey that will take us through a quiet, inner revolution: "The problems we face cannot be solved by the same level of thinking that created them."

In other words, it's our way of thinking that created the

problem in the first place! So if we keep thinking along the same lines, things will go from bad to worse. "The definition of insanity is doing the same old thing over and over again while expecting different results."[2] So try out a new idea. Life without change can become boring. That's another reason why people go on a trip; the human need to get away from the old beaten path is universal.

Keep an open mind as we move along the road less traveled. Once you give yourself permission to let go of your old way of thinking about that dispute, a mental shift will occur. That shift will be inevitable after the following 'gymnastic' cycle has been completed. We're going to turn your conflict inside out, upside down, and after a final good shake, the fall-out will surprise you. You'll feel as if you're seeing that old dispute for the first time, thus your reaction to it will be unlike your usual one.

I have journeyed along this road as a dispute mediator for more than a decade, and I am still in awe of the transforming power that radiates to the weary fighters of many battles. In my mediation work, I met Ali who was a tired, yet stubborn warrior. He was proud of his ability to fight the good fight!

ALI versus SARA

Ali waged a war against Sara, his business partner. He wanted to sue her for 'stealing' money from their company in order to advance a side business interest that she was developing in secret. He had not bothered to find out whether this extra business interest could dovetail with their existing business. He was so enraged at discovering the hole in their finances that he wanted to literally 'kick butt', shove her out the door and force her to quit! Ali's fierce anger fueled Sara's nasty counterattack. The business environment grew into a hot war zone!

When I intervened as a mediator I saw a classic case of mistrust and miscommunication. These two people had hurt each other very deeply and now just wanted revenge. When I turned the heat off Sara and Ali, they were able to redefine their dispute in objective, clear-cut terms. A shift in their thinking had occurred by the time they explored what they each valued about the business, as well as each other. Then individual needs and goals were expressed. This led to a collaboration that resulted in an agreement on their future business responsibilities.

Later, I learned that Sara's secret side interest proved to be quite profitable for their business. But in the beginning she had kept the development stage of her project undercover, because she had feared Ali's rejection due to his cautious and conservative nature. There is an old saying about something that was once broken, becomes stronger after it's mended. This was clearly the case with Ali and Sara. As they worked hard to overcome major differences, they forged a bond that was stronger than before. If two partners always agree, then perhaps one of them isn't even necessary!

The anger, mistrust and resulting miscommunication that Ali and Sara experienced are also very common in lovers' quarrels, parent-child disputes, customer-salesperson clashes, divorce fights, corporate battles, in-law brawls, friendship feuds, and this list goes on and on. The Action Plan will enable you to switch tracks – get out of the old conflict-ridden rut and stretch out onto a new road that leads to a solid solution. A readiness for change is vital to the success of this venture, which will challenge many ideas you now hold sacred. Before we travel to our starting point, we need to check that each person has warmed up for the trip ahead.

Anyone who begins this journey 'cold' is likely to give up before they reach their destination, due to the early onset of fatigue. A good pre-trip warm-up is reflected in the amount of frustration or anger that has built up in your body as a direct result of the conflict that you face. After all, it's when people feel good and angry that they get an overwhelming urge to right a wrong. A revolution needs some fiery sparks! So a certain amount of anger acts like a positive, motivating force to get you started on this trip.

HOT EMOTIONS FRY THE BRAIN!

Be careful. Feeling some anger is very different from being hot-headed. A shot of anger can be regarded as your initial fuel injection! After that your brainpower has to click in and carve out a solution that is solid. As your coach, I will help you to convert anger's negative energy into positive negotiating power. It's this kind of power that will move you forward to your desired destination.

THE ROAD AHEAD

The following comics will give you a preview of The Action Plan, by introducing you to the main activity that will occur in the six areas we will be traveling through. Regard it as your personal adventure package. Travel at your own pace.

DROP YOUR GUN!

1. Your very first step on this path marks the beginning of peace talks. The fight is over, so the people who are involved in the dispute agree to drop their guns. The term 'gun' represents any abusive verbal or non-verbal exchange – that includes sarcasm! A defensive brick wall has already been built because people automatically had to protect themselves from the previous attacks. At the end of our journey, this brick wall will have toppled, just like in a revolution!

TUNE IN

2. You and your opponent are worlds apart, so clear your reception channel and tune in to their view of the conflict. If you try to understand their story first, then they will be open to listening to you. Put your emotions into a neutral standby position, in order to avoid any unnecessary friction on the channel. This is a time to gather all the information together in order to understand the thoughts and feelings on each side.

DIG DOWN

3. We'll be rolling down a long, dark tunnel as brilliant light is focused on human needs. Many important needs lie hidden in your subconscious, so we have to dig deep down. You are about to uncover unmet needs that have driven your conflict into high gear. This discovery will create a shift in how you view the dispute. So dig boldly. Go all the way to reclaim some treasured needs.

FISH AROUND

4. Now that you know what the needs are for each party in the dispute, we fish around for solutions to meet those needs. A whole world of possibilities floats just below the surface. Fishing requires a great deal of patience and stamina. Avoid drowning in the vast ocean of emotion. Creative angling, in the form of brainstorming, is part of this process where you hook in as many potential solutions as possible. Your catch-of-the-day will be well worth the wait.

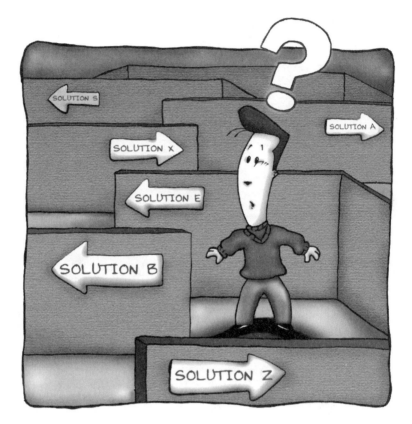

EVALUATE

5. All those possible solutions that you fished out need to be carefully weighed and dissected. Toss back the 'fishy' solutions that neither of you want. Create a maze of possibilities by labeling the leftover solutions as A, B, C, and so on. Evaluate which solutions will lead to an agreement that will meet both your needs. Be aware of superficially attractive solutions that could lead to a dead-end. When you have both agreed on the winning solution, it will take you down the right path to a formal agreement.

CELEBRATE!

6. The terms of your new agreement will be officially printed and then signed. Congratulate yourselves because you've broken through some difficult communication blocks; that old brick wall has crumbled. A difficult dispute has been solved because you honored each other's needs by collaborating in good faith. Now that you have arrived at your desired destination, it's time to celebrate! You have achieved your goal.

Regardless of WHO you are or WHAT you do, it is possible to reach an agreement. It helps if you keep your negative emotions in check.

Let the message in this sign act as a reminder that a raw outburst of anger can knock you off course within seconds.

CAUTION SIGN

Getting back on track after a derailment is possible, but the road ahead becomes riskier to travel on. After someone's angry venom has spilled out, goodwill gets poisoned. The deadly gun was exposed, thus people are on guard and turn to building communication barriers to protect themselves from the next possible attack. These barriers can sabotage the entire resolution process. As a result, I have devoted the second and third chapters to the topic of anger, which is a complex and powerful emotion. If you feel no negative emotion, such as frustration or anger, then skip ahead to chapter four where I focus on denial.

Please ignore that last part about denial; it was written tongue in cheek! Chapter four isn't about denial. I was referring to the fact that some people are in such a big rush to get on with a task, that they don't take time to honestly connect with their emotional self. They deny the existence of their hurt feelings in order to avoid pain. Escape from difficult issues comes in many forms; people may become workaholics, alcoholics, sexaholics, or shopaholics. Others live in denial because they medicate their emotional pain with a drug of their choice. I acknowledge that there are cases where a drug like Prozac can help a person get back on track. But the research shows an addiction to drugs that numb emotional pain. Sixty percent of people who manage to stop using Prozac, or a drug like it, go back on it again. Thus a drug like this can keep people prisoners in their own hell.

Thoreau coined the expression about people living lives of quiet desperation. If people keep burying their emotional selves, they will short-circuit the success of this problem solving journey.

A noted psychologist, Paul Gelinas said,
"Our society is moving towards dangerous levels of anger." [3]

The journey ahead will provide a healthy and constructive release of anger. Anger that has been denied constructive expression builds up inside until one day it spills out and hurts someone. Newspaper headlines certainly reflect such occurrences, or just look at and listen to the activity around you. I saw a driver recklessly showing off his crude style of road rage. He was driving too quickly to stop at a red light so when he slammed on his brakes, he screeched to a stop, landing part of his car on the sidewalk. A pedestrian who saw this got extremely angry at the brazen driver. This pedestrian, in turn, displayed lethal amounts of 'sidewalk rage'! The driver no longer felt safe inside the protective armor of his car as the pedestrian began banging the sharp, steely point of his umbrella on the driver's windshield. Rude gestures and noises were flying in all directions!

Before these two crazed characters met, their anger was already bubbling inside, building up pressure and looking for an outlet. Have you felt like you're on a personal collision course?! We all experience anger and it is as normal a part of life as eating and sleeping. Acknowledge your anger, and then release it through The Action Plan.

It is possible to air your anger in an honest and direct way without causing the other person to yell back or walk away. Unfortunately, most of us weren't taught how to do that. Reading and writing were considered far more important skills to learn. When conflicts did occur in our youth we were told what we must think, say and do. And as we got older we stopped taking advice from our parents and turned to our friends. We have practically been socialized to seek help from others. If our friends can't help, we seek advice on what we should do from therapists, ministers or lawyers. Dr. Frederick Covan, a chief psychologist in New York City, says that even highly successful people go to a shrink just hoping to have their conflict solved by someone else.

A conflict that has been brewing inside you for months or years, cannot be accurately summarized in five minutes or five hours! No one else can peek into the depths of your heart and mind and gain an intimate understanding of what you are going through. It's practically impossible to describe the entire history and intensity of your dispute. Plus, when talking to friends or lovers in particular, it's only human nature to describe your role in the dispute in rather innocent terms. The naked truth gets lost in the translation of the event. The person listening will not be able to walk a mile in your shoes, no matter how many times they say, "I understand." Yes, that includes even the very best therapists!

If you hire a lawyer, he will listen to your case and then add his thoughts as he plans a strategy. When you read the legal language that describes your case, you barely recognize it as your conflict. Your lawyer speaks with the other person's lawyer, who in turn tells his version of what he heard to his client. The original intent of what you wanted to say is lost. And to top it all off, you are paying big dollars for this miscommunication. You aren't even permitted to talk with your opposing party in an attempt to correct the misinformation he or she has received.

MOST IMPORTANT OF ALL

- **No solution to a conflict can occur without your receiving direct, first-hand input from the other person who's involved in it.**

- **Don't give up your control to an outsider, no matter who that person may be. The Action Plan puts the power into your hands.**

It's all up to YOU!

Here are some responses that a deeply troubled man received when he went on a quest for the right solution.

Wife: If you really love me, you'll follow my advice. I'm putting the future happiness of our marriage first.

Brother: This job is mine. As your older brother I've helped you out of tight spots before. You know I have the best solutions. We're family!

Therapist: When did you first start feeling angry at Julia? Think back to your childhood.

Mother: I know what's best for you, my boy!

Boss: This decision is mine to make. If you don't like it,...quit. I have a business to run.

Lawyer: We'll nail the sucker!

Neighbor: I know you trust me because I have years of experience in these matters. I won't steer you wrong.

Lover: No-one knows you quite like I do. I'm in touch with your sensitive side. So, here's the plan.

This same man was last seen running at full tilt to catch a plane headed for Las Vegas.

We alone have the inside track on how to best satisfy our needs. But we give up because it's hard to know where or how to begin. Yet most of us do share a longing to solve a conflict in such a way that the stressed-out relationship is restored. There are some exceptions where people don't want to continue the relationship, be it a business association, marriage or a friendship; they just want to resolve the dispute so that they can move on with their lives. It's easier to move forward when you're not dragging along old baggage.

View your conflict as a quest for the right solution. Even the most painful, gut-wrenching crisis can become a profound and richly rewarding journey. First we travel inside to discover the root cause of our conflict — those unmet needs. This knowledge will enable us to cross the great divide and collaborate with our 'opposing party'. The urge to be a peacemaker springs from deep within our human nature. Man, by nature is a social animal who yearns to get along well with others. Even the control freak wants to be loved! We also know we need to get along with the diverse cultures on this shrinking planet. But more importantly, we all feel a need "TO ACT" as opposed to "BEING ACTED UPON!" If people have dumped on you and forced their disagreeable, abusive ways of working or living on you, then you've been "ACTED UPON." So, take charge and,

BEGIN A NEW JOURNEY!

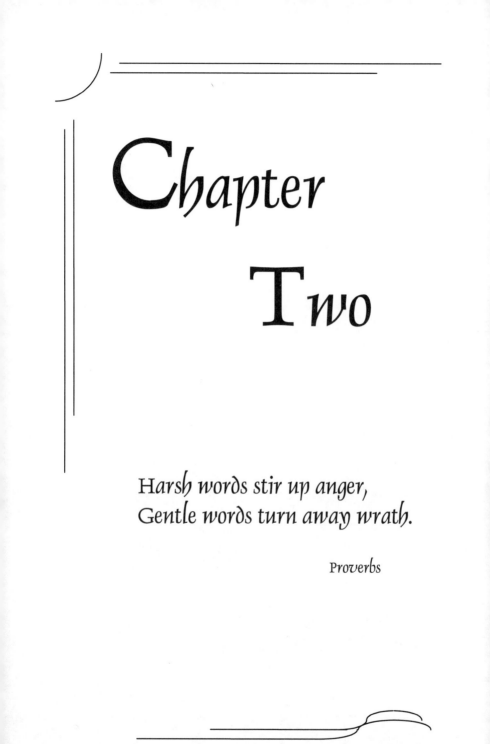

Chapter

Two

Harsh words stir up anger,
Gentle words turn away wrath.

Proverbs

Drop Your Gun

We are now in the region that has been marked, "DROP YOUR GUN." We 'gun' someone down each time we shoot our mouths off in anger; vicious verbal snipes, subtle sarcastic slurs, cynical jabs and issuing blame are just some examples of our verbal artillery. There are people who should register their tongue as a dangerous weapon! Non-verbal messages can be equally powerful; a certain look, a gesture or an intonation can strike a deadly blow at someone's pride, intelligence, judgment and self-respect. Such negative encounters slow down the progress towards peace because it keeps people in the heat of the battle. Even if you're on a low simmer, it's best to turn the heat off. A cool mind can click into neutral gear, which will make traveling over the 'hot spots' easier.

The Talmud says, "with a weapon you can kill up close, with a word from across the world." Voice-mail, e-mail, and faxes can be used as tools of electronic weaponry. E-mail was created to encourage instantaneous communication and thus lead to increased productivity. Yet the angry words that often race across the screen act as blocks to communication. A national company has installed a system that routinely searches all employee e-mail for offensive language. As soon as rude language is detected, a notice pops up on the employee's screen:

WARNING!
This is inappropriate language to use and a copy of this message will be sent to your supervisor immediately.

Some people have developed very sophisticated ways of unleashing their anger; they smile while their velvet hammer slowly pounds out a message designed to strike a person down. Such classy people don't stoop to using those common little dirty words. In the end, it doesn't matter whether you're a highbrow or lowbrow fighter, the sad truth which emerges is that our human instinct to fight is stronger than our will to make peace. Yet we all dream of world peace, even though we may have some difficulty keeping the peace in our own kitchens.

We aren't born knowing how to negotiate peaceful solutions, thus it's easy for the fighting instinct to prevail. Whether you're the one being gunned down or the one holding the smoking gun, there are no winners, and the dispute still remains to be solved. A fight just leads to a revenge attack, and then another and another. This circle of retaliation can spin relentlessly! Unresolved conflicts elevate the body's stress to levels that can be dangerous.

IS YOUR GUN POINTED AT YOUR HEART??!

It can happen! Here's how. Topping the list of illnesses that stress-triggered bullets cause is heart disease, which has become the number one killer in western countries. Your own family doctor could tell you that the stress of being angry, or even *thinking spiteful thoughts,* will make you more vulnerable to heart disease in several ways.

Heart disease begins very slowly when stress thickens blood, increases blood pressure, releases cortisone which weakens the immune system, increases cholesterol in the blood, and if you overindulge in processed snack foods to calm your edgy nerves, then you will have more fatty deposits in your arteries.

ORAL GRATIFICATION

Overeating is a classic 'flight' response to a conflict that appears impossible to solve. Many people withdraw from a bad scene and take refuge in comfort foods, which tend to have a high fat content. Others may escape via alcohol or drugs. Self-destruction usually isn't a conscious choice, but it is a possible outcome if there is no self-control.

The second classic response to conflict is to stay and fight. People in this group wage a verbal battle that could become physical. These people are the angry, 'in-your-face' types.

THE ENDLESS FIGHT

Other people resort to sly, covert fighting tactics. Their behavior sends out mixed messages, so they are hard to figure out and thus can cause us a great deal of mental angst. The vast majority of people will either stay

to fight, or take flight.

Both these reactions to conflict lead to heightened levels of stress which will cause some physiological damage. The medical facts clearly indicate that a human body cannot be constantly trying to adapt to heightened levels of stress without showing some damage.

Dr. Hans Selye, a professor of medicine and surgery at the University of Montreal, conducted many studies on the impact of stress. He proved that there is a breakdown of the body's adaptation to stress over time, and the result can be sheer exhaustion, a cold, a nervous breakdown, a collapse in the form of a heart attack, or perhaps a major illness such as cancer.

Medical research just keeps pumping out volumes of evidence that prove angry people have a higher incidence of premature deaths. Dr. Redford Williams states in his book, *Anger Kills*, "that hostile people, those with high levels of anger, cynicism and aggression, are at a higher risk of developing life-threatening illnesses." [4]

It's no wonder that the Center For Disease Control has declared anger to be a disease.

ANGER'S PROFILE

No matter what the dispute, certain common denominators emerge. Whether you're embroiled in a corporate battle, a custody fight, an insurance claim dispute or a lovers' quarrel, here is an overview of the sequence of events. First the frustration builds, then the anger flares, and by the time 'smoke' is coming out of our ears, we know something in our system has broken down. We lose control and, 'snap', out pops the gun and we spray our opponent with a shower of our angry, embittered diatribe. Those nasty words keep us in the war zone.

Let's move in for a look at the action on the battlefield. Mr. Ho has received some unacceptable merchandise, which was delivered late. So Mr. Ho grabs the phone and fires off some low down, dirty bullets at Mr. Zip, the supplier. In quick defense he puts up a communication block, refuses to listen, and begins blaming Mr. Ho for submitting an incorrect order. They take turns hurling their nasty words and personal put-downs and threatening to sue each other. Eventually they both end up feeling emotionally exhausted and beaten with no solution in sight.

Traveling to a different playing field, the marriage arena, we see a similar communication barrier being erected. He calls her a liar and a cheat, and she tells him he's a lush who can't be trusted. Their rage buries the underlying issues. They aren't ready to drop their guns, so the real reason why she felt she had to lie can't surface. For some couples, this is the only sport they play together that gets their heartbeat thumping! They become very clever at ducking and dodging each other's bullets. Those painful punches, whether verbal or physical, just keep coming. But one little mistake and the next punch could be deadly.

A relationship, whether personal or professional, can only withstand so much crossfire before it falls to pieces.

FIGHTING STYLES

Have you ever wondered why some people seem to thrive by yelling and pushing other people around, while others who may be equally angry hide their emotions? Our style of expressing emotions and resolving conflicts is established when we are very young.

Here's an example of how Sandi's parents reacted to conflict and its long-term impact on her. At the age of seven, when Sandi got angry over some dispute with her brother, her parents immediately punished her by sending her to her room. She was told it was not acceptable for her, the older sister, to get angry. At this early age she was forced to control her emotions and put her brother's needs first. She was receiving the clear message that showing anger was bad and other people's needs came first. In essence, she was receiving lifetime training on how to deny her emotions.

Twenty years later, Sandi still dreads revealing any slight form of anger. She's afraid of being rejected if she doesn't agree with other people. Sandi doesn't even acknowledge her anger to herself. As a result, a high degree of tension has built up in her body from repressed anger. This tension seeks an outlet, and finds it in the form of severe headaches.

Over the years, Sandi's inability to express her overwhelming anger and negotiate for her own needs has led to an immense sense of powerlessness and despair. She eventually had to be medicated for depression. So her 'gun' had gone off and sprayed an internal toxic spill. Her raging anger manifested itself in a silent scream.

Do you identify with someone who leads a life of quiet desperation or with the more aggressive fighter? Most of us will fall somewhere in between these two extremes. Our responses to conflict slide up and down this scale depending on who else is involved in the disagreement. The following exercise may lead you to a new perspective on your behavior.

PLAY THE CONFLICT WORD GAME!

Explore your thoughts and feelings about conflict by playing the conflict word association game. Stop to consider how you react to the word 'conflict'. Does this word stir up negative feelings or thoughts? Describe whatever your first reaction is to this word. Think back to your childhood and recall how conflicts were solved in your home. How are they solved now?
Jot down some descriptive phrases.

_____

_____

_____

_____

_____

_____

_____

_____

_____

_____

_____

What we believe about conflicts comes from the messages we have received from our parents, teachers, significant others, and the media. Parents and teachers traditionally punished children when they were embroiled in a conflict. Most of us were told what we must think, say and do. It's not surprising that many people don't trust their ability to solve conflicts and thus they seek advice from others.

THE BASIC PREMISE

The basic premise of problem-solving is that if you own the problem, then you also own the solution to it. Your solution is within your own grasp, and thus it is my job as your coach to guide you to it. Yet human nature tends to set up obstacles. Some people prefer clinging to the edge of a cliff; they'd rather be uncomfortable and struggle, day after day.

LIVING ON THE EDGE

On the other hand, there are people who find procrastination is far easier, and certainly much safer! Once upon a time, they had tried doing something about the dispute, but it didn't work out, so they have given up. Now they have begun to derive some pleasure from feeling sorry for themselves, as they blame the world out there for their woe. Some of them have quit having a life. They connect with the outside world through the safety of their remote control, as their spirit bleeds into a virtual reality.

LIVING IN A BOX

Does the person with whom you're having the conflict fit into one of the last two cartoons?

The cliffhanger and couch potato types of people will feel a little bit better if you allow them to vent <u>some</u> emotions. Watch out for their tendency to get carried away. Some of them will even look to you for help. People love being rescued. A part of us regresses to a dependent stage that is reminiscent of childhood, when others took care of our problems. We also tend to get impatient and yearn for immediate solutions.

If you provide a person with a quick-fix answer, then you'll be guilty of sabotaging the problem-solving process. Your gun will have sprayed a dirty bullet and knocked someone off the path ahead. The short-cut solution has a high degree of appeal, especially if someone close to you has been feeling helpless and distressed for a long time. The conflict has begun to wear you down, so you are seeking some relief for yourself as well.

Resist the temptation of becoming a power player by jumping in to rescue someone else! Your quick fix solution may even appear to work, at least for the short term. The other person, who was desperate for help may have such faith in your instant cure that she will bury her anger. But over time, suppressed emotions can build extra megawatts of energy that seek release in one form or another; the silent internal scream and the fight being two possibilities.

I shall restate the basic premise; anyone, who *owns a dispute*, also *owns the solution to it*. Thus the questions that appear in the problem-solving process guide a person's thinking to the solution that lies within him or her. Recognizing our ownership of a problem is important to overcoming it. If you have been a rescuer once too many times, The Action Plan will take the pressure off you. The goal is to tackle the problem in collaboration with the other person who is involved. By maintaining an atmosphere of respect and patience, the opposing parties stand a good chance of resolving their dispute. Unfortunately, our dominant culture drives us to think otherwise.

MEDIA MADNESS

The world we live in does not celebrate civilized negotiation. That's one reason why people embarking on this journey find it hard to let go of their guns. The numerous media messages that bombard us daily, urge us to carry a 'gun', hold it up high, and be ready for action! Even our friends and family may tell us to fight to the finish. And if we can't win on our own, then we call in the 'hired gun', otherwise known as a lawyer, to fight our battle for us.

Movie directors glamorize gunslinging characters who swagger and swoon over their sweet victories of revenge. After all, who would pay to see a movie where people sit down and talk in a reasonable manner in order to resolve their dispute?

Many comic books, music videos, computer and video games are informally teaching us, especially our young people, that pleasure can be derived from violence. The following is a sample description of a computer game that typically makes millions of dollars. Equip your fighter with the hottest weapons and technology that mankind has to offer. This DR13 warship, with its crazed guns, offers the most action possible in a blazing, shoot'em up game.

When this game is over and you've killed everyone in the universe, your veins continue to pump adrenaline. Your 'gun' is probably still on red alert, and you're ready to punish anyone who commits the least disturbance within your personal space.

I will sidestep the topic of **overt violence** which takes the form of dead bodies that pile up on TV, and take a sideswipe at the **covert violence** that simmers underneath the dramatic dialogue. Prime time dramas that feature actors who yell and continually put each other down are disturbing. Canned laughter is supposed to encourage us to laugh with the bully as he or she disrespects others. It appears that TV shows and movies are trying to outdo each other and break the record for tough, ill-tempered acts!

The characters in the *Seinfeld* show were very big on acting out annoyance and impatience. The word compassion was alien to them. There was a 'don't bother me' streak running through the *Seinfeld* series that revealed an inability to respond to others in appropriate ways. Robert Fulford, a Canadian journalist, described the cast as being emotionally impotent, because they never reached above the infantile stage of yelling and putting others down. This show was extremely popular, and so I have to wonder how this reflects on us as caring people.

Has the media legitimized our cruel put-downs?

The worst crime occurs when parents degrade their young children. Any child who is repeatedly called bad or stupid, will believe it and begin to act out accordingly. The world outside our doors isn't always very nice, so when a person, young or old, can't count on being respected at home, it's very sad.

BEWARE OF SARCASMITIS

'Sarcasmitis' is a disease characterized by the careless use of sarcasm. It rips off a layer from a person's dignity, leaving an invisible wound. Sarcasm is a form of anger that is used to keep people at a distance. It can slowly creep into healthy relationships and cause hurt and alienation. Television producers could put up a sign warning people that their show's heavy dose of sarcasmitis may erode your sense of decency, and that of your children. This invisible culprit can do more harm than a dozen dead bodies piled up on the screen. We all know 'thou shall not kill', but who has ever said sarcasm is bad? Common sense dictates that the messages, which repeatedly go in through the ears, will eventually come out through the mouth, unless you are a rare individual with a built in crap detector that deletes the garbage.

Multitudes of media messages sink into our subconscious and surface when we least expect them. After the shocking tragedy where numerous teenagers were gunned down by fellow students in Colorado in 1999, the power of the media to influence behavior hit home. Distributors asked US video stores to pull a specific violent film from their shelves, because it was believed to be directly linked to the teen murders. Television producers also pulled some episodes of *Buffy, The Vampire Slayer* off the air. Another movie has come under attack in a lawsuit by the parents of three students shot in Kentucky.

I hasten to point out that the media alone cannot be blamed for the existence of young criminals. There are many contributing factors. Yet one truth rings out loud and clear; the media does feed us a well-rounded diet of cruel and violent actions. Have we become so conditioned to media's vulgar messages that the pain, which we experience in our personal lives, has slipped into our comfort zone? Has our top layer of sensitivity become numb? If so, then it will take increasingly bigger jolts before we recognize that we've just been dealt a hurtful blow.

We have all been recipients of nasty, vindictive, unjust words and actions. Some words seem to crawl right into our system and 'kick against our brain.' Our natural reaction is to take flight or stay to fight. It's certainly not easy to drop our gun. It's quite remarkable how easily a finger seems to slide into the gun's trigger position. It's so effortless that it seems like an unconscious act! Basic instinct is at work.

The urge to shoot the other guy's argument to pieces has to be reckoned with sooner or later if we want to have a peaceful night of sleep. And if that other guy happens to be our life partner, our need for peaceful sleep is rather urgent!

Marriage counselors can make relatively accurate predictions about a couple's future happiness based on how well they are able to resolve conflicts. Some of them would even go so far as to say that 50 percent of all divorces could have been prevented if people had been more careful about what words came out of their mouths during a dispute. Once the wrath of anger has been unleashed, the slide downhill will be swift.

THE ORAL TRAP A

Words have the power to hurt as well as heal.

Doctors claim that if people had been more careful about what went into their mouths, 50 percent of all deaths could have been delayed significantly.

THE ORAL TRAP B

The mouth could be viewed as our ultimate source of pleasure or pain, life or death! If we control what we put into our mouth and what words come out of it, we will enjoy a healthier physical, as well as mental state.

Consider the impact of anger on our mental faculties. Each time you yell, throw something, punch or slam the door, push or hit someone, or hide your feelings by saying and doing nothing, your own self-esteem takes a beating. Deep inside, you know you blew it. You wish you could have handled the conflict differently. It still remains to be solved, which makes you feel miserable. And if a sense of hopelessness settles in, over time, depression could result. This is why I say that the gun we carry is unintentionally pointed at ourselves.

HOW DO YOU DROP YOUR GUN?

If you haven't yet reached the stage where you're sick and tired of fighting or hiding, believe me, you will eventually. There is no point in waiting for that kind of bitter end. So why put yourself through it? If your anger, whether overt or covert, highbrow or lowbrow, has already caused some wear and tear on your system, then let the healing process begin with **APEX.**

APEX

A - I ACKNOWLEDGE that my conflict need not be permanent.

P - My POSITIVE attitude prevents my anger from aggravating the conflict that I want to solve.

E - ENTHUSIASM for a final solution keeps me receptive to the thoughts and feelings of the other person.

X - I X-PEL my need to fight or take flight by being a peacemaker.

The APEX self-talk statements will build up your internal reserves of goodwill, thus making it easier to drop your gun. The tradition of self-talk has spread far and wide because it really works. Simply copy the APEX statements onto a piece of paper and keep them in your wallet. Read them over as often as you can, especially when you're in a traffic tie-up or store line-up.

The word APEX signifies the highest level attainable in any human task. Lengthy, on-going disputes could cost you a great deal – success at work or a loving relationship. So strive for your APEX – your personal best. Put the power and the glory back into your words. Those simple, everyday words that can break or heal a relationship!

Apex will launch you into The Action Plan!

Chapter

Three

> Things do not change; we change.
>
> Henry David Thoreau

> Venting anger may serve to maintain the old patterns in a relationship, thus ensuring that change does not occur.
>
> Harriet Goldhor Lerner

Heated Emotions

The biggest challenge many people face is deciding when they will be emotionally ready to sit down and solve a conflict with a person they can't stand to be near. You probably walked away from the last big argument feeling very upset, hurt or angry. It's natural to be puzzled by how the situation got out of control so quickly. Perhaps you were discussing something quite insignificant, and it just blew up into a fight that now threatens the future of your career or a special relationship.

Consider these expressions: <u>drowning</u> in rage, <u>sinking</u> into despair, and <u>falling</u> into lust. The underlined verbs indicate descending action. It's as if the rush of our emotions has intoxicated our mind and pulled us down to operate on a gut level. Functioning by raw instinct takes little effort compared to using our mental powers. Intense emotions blow out our ability to listen and think clearly.

Whenever we're fueled by an intense, negative emotion, nothing works. Many people who strive to drop their 'gun' find that even after they have begun using positive words, unpleasant and sometimes destructive emotions still surface and sabotage their best intentions. If this has happened to you, then you have been swept into the Emotional Spin Cycle.

THE EMOTIONAL SPIN CYCLE

The Spin is triggered by the excess energy that is pumped into our bodies when we experience a strong emotion like anger. To be precise, it's a rush of adrenaline that sends us flying – flying right off the handle! There are those people who get addicted to this adrenaline rush; they fly high and feel fearless. When they finally crash, watch out!

During the post-crash period, it takes very little pressure on a person's Hot Button to reactivate the Emotional Spin Cycle. A Hot Button is <u>anything</u> another person might say or do that jump-starts the spin of negative emotions. An unpleasant response pattern develops toward someone over time, so it becomes cyclical in nature.

CONNECT WITH YOUR HOT BUTTONS

To get out of your Emotional Spin Cycle, think about how your opponent manages to press your Hot Buttons so successfully. Jot down the words, phrases or actions that stir up your frustration and anger.

There is a very good chance that you will hear these same words, or see similar behaviors when you sit down to solve your conflict. Your opponent has had time to become an expert in pushing your Buttons with great skill and force.

You now have an opportunity to outsmart, or short circuit his game plan. It's possible to disconnect your Hot Buttons, so that the next time they get pushed nothing happens. In other words, the Spin Cycle won't be activated. Now the other person will no longer receive any pleasure from pushing your Buttons. Such loss of control is very disappointing, thus he will give up trying. If you feel like you've been spinning your heels in emotional slush and going nowhere fast, simply disconnect your Hot Buttons.

DISCONNECT YOUR HOT BUTTONS

This is a foolproof strategy. By associating a positive statement with an expression that angers us, <u>we can cancel</u> its original intention, which was to upset us in some way.

Sample positive statements:

1) I'm not going to let him pull my emotional strings anymore.
2) I have stopped fighting. It's great to be in charge of how I'm feeling.
3) I'm finally free of that person's control. She won't be getting any more thrills from pushing my Buttons!
4) I certainly won't grant her the privilege of pushing me around the bend again.
5) I need a life! Now I'm getting what I want by problem-solving.

Copy one or two of these phrases that you like, or write some yourself, and keep them in a handy place. Repeat them whenever you have a chance. Several repetitions a day will build up the power of your mind and enable it to zap the negative emotions that are stirred up each time your Button gets pushed. Think of your mind as a muscle. The positive statements will condition your mind to be strong, so that you will repel the 'enemy's' advances. The goal is to move off the battleground and into neutral territory where problem-solving talks can begin.

By the time your positive statements have sunk into your subconscious, you'll have created a new reality. This reality can be formed by linking your positive statements with a picture. Back in 1944, Dale Carnegie wrote about "the magical power of thought." [5] He was referring to visualization, which is how the mind forms mental pictures. We will now prepare the atmosphere in which visualization can occur successfully. This exercise will build up the power of your mental muscle even further.

VISUALIZATION

Close your door and put up a sign, 'Gone fishing!' Turn off the lights and then sit or lie down in a quiet place. Relax your body by taking a few deep breaths. Take a deep breath in to a count of seven, and then exhale to a count of seven. With your eyes closed, picture the person with whom you're having a dispute. Paint a mental picture of that person when he or she presses your Hot Buttons. The following tips will help to make your 'daydream' as real as possible.

Tips on visualization

1) Which room is this person in?
2) Where is he standing or sitting?
3) See his facial expression.
4) What shirt is he wearing?
5) Is this person chewing gum?
6) Can you smell any cologne or perfume?
7) Hear the tone of the voice.
8) Feel your Hot Button(s) being pressed.

Just as you feel some frustration or anger beginning to build, repeat one of your positive statements. If your statement was, "I'm not going to let him pull my emotional strings any more," then spend about two minutes LINKING your picture with those words. You will forge a strong link by repeatedly switching between your **words** and mental **picture**. Eventually they will merge together. Don't worry if during the first thirty seconds your thoughts jump around; most people go through a restless phase before their mind is ready to settle on the linking task.

The above exercise has incredible power because your mind doesn't know the difference between a real-life experience and a visualization of that same experience! What better way to program your mind for success? If you repeat any new thought pattern at least twenty-four times in a row, then by the twenty-fifth repetition it will have become a natural way of thinking.

Highly accomplished individuals hire personal visualization coaches to keep their mind's focus razor sharp, so they will achieve their goals. There has been an unparalleled burst of scientific data on emotion and brain imaging in the last few years. Such new discoveries help us to understand the power we each possess to bring about significant change.

Daniel Goldman's three-hundred page book, *Emotional Intelligence*,[6] clearly proves we can control our emotions. He describes the neural connections between our Hot Buttons and our brain's circuitry in highly scientific terms. The bottom line is that we can learn to control our responses to anger-provoking triggers and neutralize their effects.

There are other practical things we can do to burn out the wiring between our Hot Buttons and the Emotional Spin Cycle. The next time you feel your body pumped with extra adrenaline and you have the urge to shoot your 'gun' off, consider suppressing your fighting instinct with these cool-down exercises. If you initiate one of these exercises early enough, then your Spin Cycle won't be activated.

COOL-DOWN EXERCISES

1) Go for a brisk walk; shopping malls are great places in bad weather.
2) Climb a nearby stairwell.
3) Punch a pillow or sofa and grunt or yell all you want.
4) Write a hate letter but don't mail it.
5) Work out at a local health club (day passes are always available if you're not a member).
6) Buy a skipping rope; skip double-time.
7) Jog around a local park; wear earphones and listen to relaxing music.
8) Go for a bike ride.
9) Run on the spot, or do some jumping jacks.

FOR IMMEDIATE RESULTS TRY THIS

10) THE SIXTY SECOND BREAK

Go somewhere private, for example a washroom would be fine. While standing, bend your knees slightly and flop over from the waist so that your fingertips are close to the floor. Exhale all your breath. Inhale slowly as you return your body to its upright position. Once you are standing straight, exhale completely as you bend or arch backwards. During your exhalation, go over the positive statement you selected earlier. My favorite one is, "I'm not going to let him pull my emotional strings anymore."

The above exercise will relax your breathing and calm your central nervous system. You can count on it to refocus your mind, especially when your emotions are racing toward that crazy Spin Cycle. The mind-body connection certainly is powerful.

The Sixty Second Break is superior to a coffee break if your stress has been mounting steadily. Caffeine stimulates the release of adrenaline and increases the heartbeat and blood pressure, so skip the java jolt. The Sixty Second Break will feel so good that you may start doing it every time you're in a private space. I do it several times in airport washrooms during long waits because it promotes a relaxed, creative frame of mind. Before repeating the exercise I pause to breathe normally a couple of times. I alter my positive statement to reflect a current stress-provoking situation, which may have nothing to do with conflict. It is such a simple and natural way to prepare for an upcoming challenge. It promotes a great sense of emotional wellbeing.

Did you know that the **vast majority** of people who walk into a doctor's office complain of illnesses, aches and pains that have been caused by emotional stress? The human body has difficulty adapting to high levels of stress. Any intense negative emotion like anger depletes the body of its vital energies. People who are going through a stressful time will complain of being tired all the time. They get sick easily because their body's immune system is low. How has anger affected you or the person with whom you're having the dispute?

Since anger is the most common emotion we associate with conflict, let's look at the Science of Anger.

ANGER'S FIVE PHASES

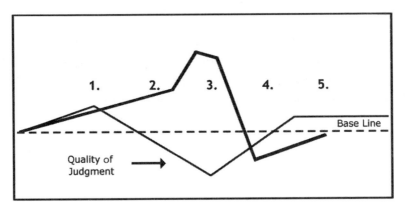

1. Trigger Phase   **3.** Crisis Phase

2. Escalation Phase   **4.** Recovery Phase

5. Resolution Phase

The upper, slightly heavier line on the graph represents the build-up and release of anger. The bottom line shows the quality of judgment that is likely to be present during each phase. Note that during the Crisis Phase, which occurs in the number three area, the quality of judgment dips to an all time low.

PHASE ONE

The TRIGGER PHASE is pretty self-explanatory; it refers to the conflict situation that triggered or caused the anger in the first place. It is time to disconnect your Hot Button.

PHASE TWO

In the ESCALATION PHASE, the breathing rate speeds up, the vocal volume gets louder, the heartbeat accelerates and muscular tension builds. The body is getting ready for a fight. The Emotional Spin Cycle has begun. If your body is in this phase, then make an exit immediately and go through some cool-down exercises.

Glance at the chart and notice how quickly the quality of judgment is rolling downhill in this phase. You're on a sinking ship! If the person you are with has just entered this phase, then try to de-escalate his anger by using non-threatening words and a calm voice. Relax your body language, and perhaps extend an open palm toward him; this being a classic peace gesture. Explain that you feel this situation is getting out of hand, so you need some time to cool down. Say it, even though it's the other person who needs to cool down. Assure him a good solution can be worked out if the two of you were to sit down later to talk calmly. Before you walk away, work out a time when the two of you could meet.

If you see that your opposing party is breathing quite rapidly as well as yelling, step back at least three feet and turn your body to a forty-five degree angle when facing this person. This will protect your vital organs from any kind of sudden, unexpected attack.

NO ONE IS IMMUNE TO VIOLENCE! NO ONE!

A close friend of mine had her ribs fractured by the most unlikely person! A man she cared about was angry about something she had done, but he'd never been the violent type. She was sitting in front of him and trying to remain composed as he yelled at her. Suddenly he stood up and lunged at her, punching her chest a couple of times. After the first punch, she was too shocked to do anything – like run away.

She never thought it could happen to her in such a sedate

and civilized environment. After the second swift punch, she managed to get out, but by then it was too late. She had become a victim of bottled-up anger that suddenly erupted. The guy had simply 'snapped'! My friend's broken ribs came very close to causing a collapsed lung. She still struggles through each day with chronic chest pain.

In a recent survey conducted by the Society for Human Resources Management, one-third of the respondents stated that one or more violent acts had been committed in their offices during the last five years; eighty percent of those incidents occurred during the last three years. The violent events described included fist fights, physical struggles and a variety of thrown objects.

I must stress that a very blurry line exists between anger's Phase Two and Phase Three. You alone are the best judge regarding what your next move should be. If in doubt, simply walk away from a bad situation.

PHASE THREE

In the CRISIS PHASE, the actual fight or assault occurs. The blood is pumped away from the brain and redirected to the muscles, so it's not surprising that the quality of judgment is at an all-time low at this point. Eighty percent of hearing is lost, thus there is absolutely no point in talking or even screaming at your opponent. By yelling "FIRE!" you might enlist outside help.

PHASE FOUR

During the RECOVERY PHASE the body is regaining its normal functioning levels. It will take some time for the person to recover from his or her high state of emotional and physical arousal. Any kind of comment could trigger another crisis, so let that person be alone.

After a couple of hours, it would be safe to check whether this person has calmed down. A simple question could be asked about how he or she is feeling.

PHASE FIVE

By the time a person reaches this final RESOLUTION PHASE, it is common for him to feel remorseful. Young people might feel frightened over their complete loss of control. There is a need to come to terms with what has happened, so the channels are usually wide open for listening and talking. A resolution process can begin only if <u>both</u> parties are ready to talk.

It would be an ideal world if we all recognized the signals that lead the Trigger Phase into the Escalation Phase. By reacting appropriately to some early danger signals, we can prevent the Crisis Phase from taking place. The attack, be it verbal or physical, couldn't occur because you have walked away.

People believe that they will instinctively know when to walk or run to safety. Unfortunately, mistakes happen. In one of North America's more civilized, large cities, Toronto, Canada, three new domestic assault courts opened in 1997. Far too many families are ripped apart as a result of uncontrolled anger.

Some people are able to mask their rage very well, right up to the last second, when suddenly they can't contain their inner 'combustion' anymore, and a shocking explosion occurs. Thus be on the lookout for the signals of the Escalation Phase in the other person. If they are breathing quickly, yelling and you see a fist forming, watch out. With experience, you will be able to move *directly* from the Trigger Phase into the final Resolution Phase, leaving out the three destructive phases that lie in between. Those three phases could be described as the build-up to the fight, the fight and the aftermath of the fight.

We were born into this world to help each other, not to hurt each other. We need each other. Let's stress the importance of 'us-centered' thinking over 'me-centered' thinking. Together we are much stronger. The problem-solving process begins with 'I' statements, and progresses to the final agreement stage, where 'we' statements get signed on the dotted line. The people involved in a dispute are the only ones who are responsible for living out the terms of their agreement. Thus they are best suited to defining their terms *together*.

The process of collaborating together is central to The Action Plan. The questions in The Plan have been designed to promote an all-encompassing discussion. It will be easier to connect with that other person after you have disconnected your Hot Buttons. Be ready for surprises. I once met a person who found a way of pushing Hot Buttons I didn't even know I owned! This is not likely to happen during the conflict resolution meeting when you are mentally prepared for the other person's aggressive moves.

The average person will probably experience the Trigger Phase of the Anger Cycle several times a week. Most 'trigger' situations will arouse feelings of frustration and anger. So it is a good idea to also rewrite your positive statement in such a way that it no longer refers to a specific situation, but has a general application. Statements 2 and 5 on page 62 already have such a broad-spectrum application. When a positive statement becomes your belief it will trigger the satisfactory feeling of being in control. Enjoy the distinct pleasure of being able to choose your reaction to a negative trigger or stimulus.

Earlier in this chapter, I suggested that you spend two minutes linking your positive statement with a mental picture till they merge into one. This method of visualization is the single most powerful tool for preparing you to talk with that difficult person. It is easy to visualize because we think in images, not in words – words are only symbolic representations of specific images. Go ahead and direct your 'mini-movie'. New opportunities lie waiting to be exposed in your mind.

Chapter Four

If there is no way out, the best course of action is to find a way further in.

Orania Papazolou

Why Mediate?

Mediation is the method of solving conflicts that has the highest rate of satisfaction when compared to more traditional methods, for example, arbitration, litigation, and plain old yelling! In Chicago Illinois, during one fifteen-month period, mediation centers handled 3,947 disputes. More than 82 percent of those disputes were successfully resolved, and as many as 95 percent for a certain category of those disputes.[7] In court you have a 50 percent chance of winning your case. Courts don't resolve disputes; they basically determine guilt and punishment, and to many people that constitutes a solution because it satisfies their anger.

If your dispute doesn't require arbitration or litigation, what other choices exist? You may pursue the coin toss, a battle of wills, a duel, a scream fest, and if these inexpensive methods don't satisfy, then what? In *When Talking Makes Things Worse*,[8] David Stiebel states that if you just try talking it out, the problem often gets worse because you don't have a strategy.

This book is focused on the interest-based strategy of mediation, which means that the opposing parties explore their respective interests, and then solutions begin to emerge from where those interests overlap. The next chapter will explore this strategy in great detail. Legal disputes are never just about *legal issues* – basic human interests and needs are at stake. A lawyer will make sure that the agreement protects your legal rights. Interest-based mediation builds a collaborative spirit, which couldn't occur in litigation where a judicial contest is being waged.

MEDIATION

If you hire a mediator, then that person is regarded as an outside, **neutral** party who will guide you and the other person to a solution. A mediator will not tell you who is right or wrong. The word neutral is key, because the mediator does not act as a judge.

The mediator controls the meeting by asking strategic questions to structure the thinking process through to a solution that both sides of the dispute can accept. The two parties are responsible for making all the important decisions along the way.

The final agreement is prepared as a legally binding contract. It is written in plain English, often quoting the very words you have used to describe the conditions of your agreement. You certainly won't have to hire a lawyer to interpret any tricky legal jargon. The agreement may also be drawn up as a non-legal document.

When I'm asked to mediate a conflict, it has usually advanced to a crisis stage and a legal battle has been threatened. I believe if my clients had tried mediation in the early stages, the conflict wouldn't have flared into such a nasty fight. So it is my hope that you will be able to solve your future disputes early, when they're still small and manageable. Nip them in the bud. Another sub-title for this book could have been, DO-IT-YOURSELF MEDIATION. My prime reason for writing this book is to assist you in solving conflicts without hiring a mediator. The outline of your mediation meeting is on page 84.

TIPS FOR DO-IT-YOURSELF MEDIATION

Select the location for your mediation meeting very carefully. I suggest that you find a lovely, quiet restaurant where there is a lot of space between the tables. This will ensure that your conversation will be relatively private. A restaurant nicely fulfills the requirement of holding the meeting in a neutral territory. A common fear centers on what happens if one person loses control and becomes loud and aggressive. Few people would dare make a public spectacle of themselves in an upscale restaurant. Plus, you never know who may just happen to walk in the door.

In a restaurant setting it's less likely that one of you will storm out prematurely when you have a meal to finish! Consider meeting in an oriental restaurant where they serve a six course meal in tiny, delicate dishes. Relaxing background music and good food will foster a calm mood, which is essential for your meeting. However, if the need should arise, you can retreat to a washroom for a Sixty Second Break.

The most popular four-letter word that begins with an "F" is....... Free. And that represents a great attraction to DO-IT-YOURSELF MEDIATION.

It doesn't cost a penny. You are only required to bring two things to the mediation table, an abundance of goodwill and patience.

The last chapter guides you in initiating mediation with the person who is involved in your dispute. I advocate starting off with DO-IT-YOURSELF MEDIATION, and if things don't work out, you can always hire a mediator.

An outstanding feature of mediation is that it's time effective. A mediation meeting can usually be planned within two weeks, and it only takes from three to six hours to complete the mediation process. Some disputes require less time. Compare this to the average one-year waiting period for a court trial. Once a trial starts, it can go on indefinitely.

Legal battles, in or outside a courtroom, have been known to continue for as long as additional 'dirt' can be uncovered about the parties involved. Due to the combative nature of the 'win or lose' legal fight, dirt has been known to fly fast and furiously! Witnesses are trotted in to defame and possibly destroy someone's character.

It's no wonder that some people are afraid to do anything

at all when faced with a serious dispute. The fear of losing their reputation can immobilize them. There is absolutely no room for any kind of mudslinging in mediation. The two parties work at building goodwill and trust by collaborating together.

Mediation is focused on moving *forward* to resolve a conflict. Litigation and arbitration, on the other hand, emphasize looking *backward*, examining who did what to whom and how often the dirty deed was done. When so much time is spent in fault-finding, whether through character assassination or other means, a great deal of negative energy and tension build up.

Mediation provides a release of tension, partly because the communication and understanding between the opposing parties improve as mutual interests are discovered. Again in sharp contrast, during and even after a court trial the communication between the two people remains blocked, and often hostile. Instead of solving a dispute, the courts are primarily concerned with establishing guilt through a win/lose fight.

Mediation is unique in that it fulfills our basic human need for respect and dignity in the resolution of difficult disputes.
For example, if one person experiences difficulty discussing a sensitive issue, a mediator can be asked to intervene. During one wrongful dismissal case where there were several issues to sort out, the woman who had lost her job was not able to tell her boss, face to face, that he was a racist. So during our caucus, which is a private meeting in another nearby room, she asked me to introduce this subject back at the mediation table. Skillful questioning of the boss's actions brought him around to the realization that his actions had been prejudiced.

This man may not have admitted to such a truth if everyone present hadn't signed a confidentiality agreement. Confidentiality is key in opening up the channels for some honest communication. In order to settle a dispute, you need to tell the whole story, not just some pretty version of it out of fear that certain facts may be used against you later on, or printed in a newspaper.

On the other hand, any matter that is settled in court becomes publicly available. And reporters who cover the legal news know where to dig to find all kinds of information to spice up an otherwise boring story.

Initially, a mediator may do more of the talking than the opposing parties, but towards the end, the two disputants practically take over! Mediators fix a communication breakdown; while there are lawyers who will feed off of such a breakdown.

A communication breakdown has definitely occurred when one person says to another, "Have your lawyer call my lawyer." Many lawyers will take unfair advantage of the anger at this opportune moment, and play it up for all it's worth – to prolong a court trial and hence make more money. Anyone who operates out of anger loses their perspective. And the buildup of tension makes it feel like your life is hanging from a tight knot, and you have no control over which way the rope is yanked.

The Human Yo-yo

No one can yank you around after your anger has cooled off. Your ability to reason will put you in charge of making decisions. That's why mediation can begin only after the 'fight' is over.

Yet the instinct to fight can sneak up on us and catch us off guard. Before you tumble into the next round of your 'fight', be it in a classroom, boardroom or bedroom, remember you can save yourself a great deal of personal grief and financial woe by considering mediation.

The fee that an individual pays a mediator has always been lower than that paid to a lawyer. That's not because the mediator charges a lower fee. It reflects the fact that both you, and your opposing party, share the cost of one mediator. In litigation, you alone pay for your lawyer's fees, so the cost will be double. Of course there are some mediators who will charge a lower hourly rate than lawyers, and the reverse of that occurs as well. Volunteer mediators are available in more and more schools, businesses and community centers.

Your conflict will become a catalyst for positive change when you move it through the mediation process, with or without a mediator present. Even if you happen to get temporarily stuck at some point during the process, more good will have come out of your discussions up to that point, than the fighting that preceded mediation.

Mediation offers a real sense of accomplishment, because in this process you have the power to make the important decisions in your life. You will have solved your own dispute! This strong sense of personal ownership of your resolution is what accounts for the extremely high success rate of mediated disputes. Why allow a distant judge, or two combative lawyers, to do your dealing for you? Why give them that kind of power? WHY?

In litigation you don't have the legal right to bring up all the facts or feelings that you think are relevant to your case! Yet decisions will be made for you, which will be based on limited evidence. We are talking about decisions that may have a big impact on the rest of your life. You can't count on a fair settlement that way. Mediation allows *you* to be the judge.

If you decide to seek your resolution through mediation today, then ten years from now you won't be beating yourself up, wondering what else you could have or should have done. A judge's decision isn't intended to solve a dispute. It often does little more than point out who had more money to hire a better lawyer and last longer in court. Yet a judge's decision is final, whereas at the end of a mediation you are free to walk out and reject the final outcome if you feel it's not fair.

YOU ARE THE BEST JUDGE OF WHAT IS RIGHT FOR YOU!

People who have experienced a courtroom trial have told me that they've felt like bystanders, throwing money into a bottomless pit while lawyers fought with each other. If you've had a similar misfortune, then you would agree with Judge Hand, who had this to say in an address to the New York Bar Association, "I should dread a lawsuit beyond almost anything else short of sickness and death." [9]

In January 1999, The Ontario government initiated Mandatory Mediation in order to encourage early settlement of a case, so it won't end up in court. Civil cases are being referred to government-approved mediators for mediation. The Mandatory Mediation HOTLINE (416-314-8356 or 1-888-377-2228) states that its goal is to save the public time and money by encouraging an early resolution. It's also a way of clearing up the backlog of cases waiting for trial. The reason why I'm on the government's roster of mediators is because I believe mediation is the superior route to justice. Everyone's voice gets a fair hearing.

I now return to the title of this chapter: "WHY MEDIATE?" Up to this point, I've described the mediation process as being quick, inexpensive, and confidential. Other attributes that make it outstanding are fairness, an historically high rate of success and personal ownership of the solution.

Here is another answer to the question, "WHY MEDIATE?" I shall repeat the opening quote for this chapter, "If there is no way out, the best course of action is to find a way further in." Mediation represents that *way* of traveling inside to where your solution lies.

The primary benefit of mediation is embedded in the subtext of this chapter. It's an aspect of the human condition that cannot be easily measured by others. But once you reach a satisfying closure to your dispute, you'll feel a special kind of peace for which the human soul searches. Attaining peace of mind is a significant achievement which begins with the inward journey.

Chapter

Five

For every thousand people hacking away at the leaves of evil, there is but one striking at the root.

Henry David Thoreau

Preparing For Success

Success never *just happens*! Think back to an accomplishment that made you feel particularly proud. Most likely you persevered through a variety of challenges, unwilling to quit. A clearly defined goal was what kept you on track. It's the same with solving a conflict. Success is dependent on having prepared your desired goal in advance.

> If you don't know what you want, there's
> a very good chance you'll never get it!

If there is no commitment to a goal, a person may not even be motivated to stick around long enough to complete The Action Plan, which consists of the six step mediation process. This process becomes meaningful once the benefits of achieving a goal are deeply felt. Passion energizes you and keeps you focused on moving forward.

Here is an overview of the mediation process.

> STEP ONE: Agree to follow the ground rules (pg. 111). They promote a positive problem-solving atmosphere.

> STEP TWO: Exchange your thoughts and feelings about the dispute.

> STEP THREE: Explore unmet interests and needs. Determine common ground. Discuss goals.

> STEP FOUR: Brainstorm for solutions that address the interests and needs of both parties.

> STEP FIVE: Evaluate the solutions and then select one with which both parties can agree.

> STEP SIX: Prepare a contract that both parties will sign. Discuss follow-up plans.

The third step is the most important one. The final agreement will be good *only if* it addresses the goals that surfaced in step three. A goal encompasses both legal rights and human needs and interests. Some inter-personal disputes will not involve legal rights.

GOAL CREATION

A goal is not a fixed point. Think of it as a *flexible circle* within which a range of agreements could occur. It is a good idea to create this circle of possibilities a week before your mediation meeting. Ideas take time to shape and jell, to expand and synthesize. There's probably a line you wouldn't consider crossing in order to achieve your goal, so define that boundary. Roll up your sleeves and begin forming your goal.

The solution sphere - you shape your boundaries.

There would be no dispute if needs were being met, so a goal statement clearly reveals the unmet needs. An entire book could be written about the wide variety of human needs, both conscious and subconscious. The words below will give you an idea of what some of our basic needs are.

NEEDS

fairness... security... privacy...
respect... equality... trust...
satisfaction... accomplishment...
acceptance... love... recognition...
economic well-being... control over
one's life... being taken seriously...
being listened to... being understood.

If you have decided to go for DO-IT-YOURSELF MEDIATION, you may find yourself talking to someone who needs a lot of help and encouragement. This person, whom you have invited to the mediation table, may have trouble expressing her needs. You could make it easier for her by showing the above list of needs, and asking which ones she identifies with. Perhaps point out a need that you have in the context of this dispute that you've come together to solve. For business disputes, there is a list of additional needs in the Endnotes.[10]

During the mediation meeting, be aware that the other person may need extra time to sort out her needs. If you are ready to move on and begin to feel restless, then excuse yourself from the room for a few minutes. Your absence will take the pressure off the other person to give you a quick answer. The importance of completing the third step thoroughly is critical to the success of the next three steps.

MORE ABOUT STEP THREE

When a dispute occurs, it's easy to get caught up with the surface issues and not even consider looking beyond them to uncover exactly which UNMET needs are driving the conflict into high gear. Here's an example of what I'm talking about.

Most of us can relate to family feuds more easily than corporate battles so my example involves Ann, who is eighteen years old, and her younger sister Sue. They're having a real cat fight because Ann has just discovered that Sue took her brand new silk blouse and wore it to a party. To top it off, Sue brought it back with a stain on it. Sue hadn't bothered asking for her sister's permission to wear the blouse. The stain was right by the front collar. Ann had planned to wear the silk top that very night when she had a date with a special guy.

The surface conflict has to do with the stain on the blouse, which was taken without permission. But if we probe beneath the obvious problem and uncover some unmet needs, then we can view the dispute differently.

Sue claims that being the younger sister has meant that she has received second-hand clothes from Ann for as long as she can remember. So she expresses a need for her *fair* share of new clothes in the family. Sue felt so jealous and angry about this unfair history that she just took the blouse. It's going to be hers one day anyway; why wait for that day to arrive?

This dispute shattered Ann's trust in her sister.

Consequently, Ann needs to gain back some trust. She also needs to feel a greater sense of respect, because she felt like her sister walked all over her.

In order to solve the conflict over the silk top, we must *first* look at ways in which the underlying needs can be addressed. Every conflict operates on at least the two levels shown in the following chart.

LEVELS OF CONFLICT

SURFACE ISSUES	A blouse has been taken without permission. It's stained and not wearable for a special occasion.
UNDERLYING NEEDS	One person needs more fairness, and the other needs respect.

If the deeper human needs are met, then the surface issues of the conflict will not keep recurring in different ways.

EXPLORE YOUR NEEDS

It's easy to lose touch with what our needs really are. Have you ever felt angry, or just disgruntled, and not been able to express what it was that you needed? As we get older, and it doesn't matter what our current age is, our needs keep changing. Thus it's good to take some time out to catch up with ourselves, by taking a personal inventory.

Review the needs listed on page 85; they will point you in the right direction. If several needs surface then rank them in the order of importance. Think about how you would like to have those needs met. For example, if your conflict was triggered by a deep need for more security, then state in specific terms how that could come about.

Let's consider the feud between the sisters that was described earlier. If Sue isn't specific about how her needs could be met at the very beginning, then the door is left wide open to many possibilities. To ensure a satisfactory outcome she will have to prepare a couple of proposals for the mediation session. She may request a weekly clothing allowance for the next few months. Ann will probably request that Sue pay for the dry cleaning bill, and promise to never walk out with her clothes again. The sisters are now moving in the right direction with some help from their parents.

Family feuds can get nasty as people waste a great deal of energy and time in attacking each other, instead of tackling the problem. Here is another approach to uncovering those critical needs that can seem so elusive.

SLIPPING UNDER ANGER

When we peel back the heavy-duty layer of anger, secondary, *simmering* emotions become visible. These emotions play a vital role in heating up anger. Many significant human needs get buried under an avalanche of powerful emotions, especially anger. When our frustrations over a dispute begin to boil over, and anger leaps onto center stage, it's time to make an exit down through a trap door.

The world underneath represents your subconscious region. Picture this space as being filled with **SECONDARY EMOTIONS** that are floating around. By selecting one or two of them that describe how you feel about the conflict, you will create a healthy distance from anger. Figure out which unmet needs have generated these secondary emotions. For example, if you selected the secondary emotion of feeling abandoned, then it could mean that there's an unmet need for acceptance. Elaborate on your unique needs regarding acceptance. By digging a little deeper, you may realize that you also have a need to be taken seriously and thus to be understood better. By weaving these thoughts together, you're creating an in-depth understanding of your dispute. This will lead you forward toward a solution more quickly than if you had stayed stuck in anger. The following list shows numerous secondary emotions. Say each word to yourself as you weigh it on your emotional scale to see if it registers any connection to an ongoing dispute in your life. Emotional weight is registered by your quiet, inner voice that responds with a heartfelt "YES" after you say a particular word. Check-mark those words.

SECONDARY EMOTIONS
THAT HEAT UP ANGER!

Abandoned	Dominated	Overwhelmed
Abused	Foolish	Remorseful
Ambivalent	Frenetic	Sad
Betrayed	Frightened	Scared
Blamed	Embarrassed	Startled
Bored	Grief-stricken	Stepped-on
Burdened	Helpless	Stupid
Challenged	Hurt	Suspicious
Cheated	Ignored	Tense
Condemned	Imposed upon	Threatened
Confused	Inadequate	Thwarted
Conspicuous	Intimidated	Tired
Cornered	Isolated	Trapped
Crushed	Jealous	Tricked
Defeated	Lonely	Uneasy
Despairing	Low	Unloved
Disappointed	Manipulated	Unsettled
Diminished	Tense	Used
Discontented	Threatened	Vulnerable
Distracted	Nervous	Worried

Explore the emotions you have check-marked by writing about the needs that tie in with them. You may discover some needs that have been suppressed for a long time. Your free-flowing thoughts, written down in journal style, will provide you with rich insights. This kind of soul searching helps to create an accurate goal statement for the mediation meeting.

Thoreau said, "For every thousand people hacking away at the leaves of evil [that is, conflict], there is but one striking at the root." The root in this case is the *underlying need*. May you uncover the real source of the conflict you face.

THE LANGUAGE OF MEDIATION

I ended chapter two by saying that our words have the power to break or heal a relationship. The manner in which we are to communicate is spelled out in the opening ground rules. These rules on page 111 promote a productive, problem-solving atmosphere. If there's an angry outburst, then valuable time and energy are wasted because it takes a while to reduce the tension. If you have hired a mediator, why pay for a needless detour away from achieving your goal?

There are many common communication blocks that slow down the mediation process. If your conversation includes position statements, an impasse will occur almost immediately!

POSITION STATEMENTS

Position statements begin with words like, "You must never..." or "You will have to..." These are harsh and inflexible statements. The other person will feel put-down and thus he will automatically become defensive. In effect, you will have pushed the other party up against your rigid wall. There's not much room for negotiation left here, because you have just 'gunned down' the spirit of collaboration.

A wide variety of interests support every position statement. During DO-IT-YOURSELF MEDIATION, if you hear a position statement, explore why the other person put it forward by seeking to understand their underlying interests. That approach should get you back on track and prevent you from getting entangled in positional bargaining. Whenever you argue over position statements, you get locked into a battle of wills and quickly end up at a dead-end. Take a look at following diagram:

Position statements can't be reconciled, but interests can.

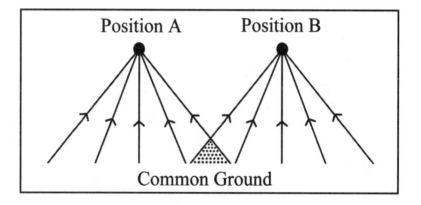

Each position statement, represented by the dot under Position A and Position B respectively, is supported by umbrella-like spokes. Individual interests, or needs, travel up the spokes, thereby feeding and shaping each position statement. In other words, position statements are created by a variety of interests. The area where these interests overlap is illustrated by a pattern of dots. A more formal name for this area is common ground.

Here's an example of positional bargaining from the political arena. In the early 1960s, talks broke down completely between President Kennedy and the Soviet Union on the topic of nuclear proliferation. The conflict centered on how many on-site nuclear arms inspections the Soviet Union and the United States should be allowed to make within each other's territory per year. The Soviets insisted on three and the Americans countered with no less than ten. Neither side gave in, and a great deal of resentment and anger resulted from their rigid position statements.

A mediator would have taken the focus away from their deadlocked positions by asking each side to describe how they would plan to carry out these inspections. Their responses would have probably revealed that they both shared an interest in not having the inspections become excessively intrusive and lengthy. Such a mutual interest would have created common ground.

Another area of common ground would be their joint interest in having the world remain safe from nuclear fallout. A goal in mediation is to discover as much common ground as is possible, so that the 'opposing' parties may begin to feel like they're on the same team, seeking solutions for common problems. There's nothing like the spirit of collaboration to motivate solid solutions.

The more interests you are able to generate, the greater the chance that some of those interests will overlap to form a sizable common ground from which shared problems emerge that require a joint resolution. Examine minor interests that, at first glance, may have no connection to the dispute being mediated.

MINOR INTERESTS can play a major role.

It is surprising how a minor interest can actually create a path to an innovative solution. I explored minor interests during a mediation that involved the payment of a large debt by a man who was not strong financially. I learned that the debtor had an incredible range of computer programming skills. He had done freelance work for some major clients. It turned out that the other party needed some computer work done, so some phone calls were made to check the work references of the debtor. His reputation as a computer programmer was very good. In the end, a final agreement was drawn up that spelled out the details of the computer work that would be provided for free, in exchange for a reduced amount of the debt.

TO BLAME OR NOT TO BLAME!

In STEP TWO of the mediation process, when the parties are exchanging their views about the dispute, blame has a tendency to sneak in the back door. Many people begin a sentence with the words, "I feel" in order to avoid blaming the other person. It is important to describe the unacceptable action immediately, for example, "I feel angry when I see all those dirty dishes piled up in the sink." In this way you aren't attacking the person but an action. This makes a *very big difference* to the person listening to you. If they feel you're directing blame at them personally, then their defensive wall goes up, and another communication impasse occurs.

Any statement that begins with, "You make me feel so _____" is a blaming statement. You are blaming someone directly for how you feel. Saying, "I feel you are being too controlling." is also a blaming statement. Remember to follow the words 'I feel' with how you personally feel. Consider these alternative ways of expressing negative emotion safely.

First, I'll tackle the example of someone getting blamed for being too controlling. It is a serious short-coming; one which needs to be addressed. Try to be more objective and factual. Describe specific behaviors that are controlling. For example, you could say, "When you make decisions without consulting me, I feel discounted and frustrated because I don't have any input about important issues." Now the facts and feelings are there, and the other person knows exactly what is bothering you. When someone you have to associate with in business hears your carefully phrased concern, that person may even warm up to you! It might be the very first time that someone has gone to this much trouble, pointing out something that has in fact always secretly annoyed her as well.

Here is a basic communication model that will prevent you from blaming a person directly, but will still make it clear that you would like to see a change occur.[11] Fill in the blanks with whatever is most appropriate for you.

A NONBLAMING COMMUNICATION MODEL

"WHEN_____(DESCRIBE WHAT UPSETS YOU), I FEEL _____(STATE YOUR EMOTION), BECAUSE _____. WHAT I WOULD LIKE FROM YOU NOW IS _____ _____ _____. IN THE FUTURE, WOULD IT BE POSSIBLE FOR YOU TO _____?"

I have now filled in the above blanks to illustrate a useful way of issuing a nonblaming statement.

"WHEN I receive your unedited newsletter, I FEEL upset, BECAUSE it's not my job to act as your editor. WHAT I WOULD LIKE FROM YOU NOW IS a response indicating that you understand why I'm upset. (Wait for their response.) IN THE FUTURE, WOULD IT BE POSSIBLE FOR YOU TO do a complete and thorough edit of this newsletter?"

A key principle of mediation is to look for solutions, not blame. In other words, look forward not backward. There is no use in blaming people because they choose to operate under rules that differ from yours. Appreciate differences because they can work for you. Many business contracts get signed precisely because people have totally opposite beliefs. A buyer of stocks believes the price will go up, and the seller of those very same stocks believes the price will go down. Both walk away from their agreement feeling happy. Make a decision about how to interact with that person whose differing values and beliefs may have hurt you. You can feel like a victim and wallow in self-pity and sympathy from others. Or, you can turn away from your preoccupation with what others are doing, or not doing, and concentrate instead on having your needs met.

THE TIT FOR TAT GAME

A person can be easily seduced into playing this game, which leads to a communication impasse. The one rule of this game states that you are to treat others in the same way that they have treated you. Many people feel a glorious high after they've 'slammed' someone right back who was rude to them first. Our fighting instinct lures us into this seductive dance.

It's an *emotional* experience of short-lived satisfaction. To prevent tit for tat, keep your mind on the long-term satisfaction of achieving your goal. You could write your goal statement on brightly colored paper and keep it in front of you. It may help deter you from playing this self-defeating game.

If you have planned to initiate DO-IT-YOURSELF MEDIATION, you won't have the benefit of having an outside person steer you away from tit for tat tangles. Keep chapter six of this book open in front of you, thus you can refer to it like a roadmap every time your instinct attempts to pull you off course.

During the mediation meeting, be aware of the rate of your verbal exchange. When a situation heats up and becomes emotional, the pace of give and take speeds up. You wouldn't want to quickly blurt out whatever comes to your mind first, especially when in the midst of mediating a business or separation agreement. By taking a break, everyone will have a chance to cool off and slow down. While on your break, try to predict how the other person will respond to what you want to say next. Will their reaction take you closer to your desired outcome or further from it? If necessary, rephrase your thought before speaking.

In the chart below, number one illustrates a collision. Before the first action (spoken thoughts) has been completed, the reaction (from the listener's side) has bumped into the conversation, thereby preventing it from moving forward.

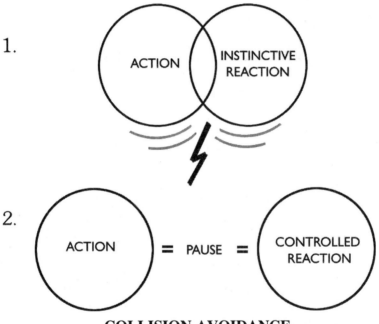

COLLISION AVOIDANCE

If a pause is built in-between the action and reaction, tit for tat won't occur as easily. Here are some ideas for filling in the pause: count to five, leave for a Sixty Second Break, make a phone call, or paraphrase what you heard in your own mind or out loud.

The pause is particularly effective just after someone has 'slammed' you. Don't stoop to responding to a dirty game they want to play. By pausing, you'll diffuse some of their negativity.

Let it all bounce off your **mental** armor!

Your self-control will translate into self-respect. Become psychologically bullet proof! Your mind is a muscle; exercise it with those positive statements that appeared on page 62. Show your strength to the other person who is pumped up for a cheap thrill. Strive to maintain an atmosphere where peace talks can take place by avoiding the communication blocks created by tit for tat, positional bargaining, and issuing blame. An open, respectful attitude will promote the exchange of intimate exposures.

INTIMATE EXPOSURES!

One reason why a mediation session takes a minimum of two or even three hours is that a fair chunk of time is needed for people to lower their defenses, and build up their levels of trust so that intimate exposures can occur. Once you have opened up and let the other person in on what your needs and private interests are, then you will have let yourself be known in a rather intimate way, hence the term, intimate exposures. The exposed picture isn't always pretty, thus some courage is necessary.

Most people won't put their ego into their back pocket very willingly. Consider the number of hours the average person dedicates to polishing their self-image so they can hold it up in a good light. But if you initiate an intimate exposure, you'll have opened the door for the other person to follow. For instance, if you are worried sick and on the brink of bankruptcy, just lay that card on the table. What do you really have to lose? There is a great deal of power in truth. People are touched by it even if they do not show it openly.

We are more alike than different; unfortunately fear and pride get in the way. Don't become a victim of your own pride. By being honest and exposing your underlying needs, you are motivating the other person to join in on the dig for solutions.

If you pause long enough to cool off,

then dig down,

common ground

will abound!

Remember Thoreau who said, "Only one in a thousand people will strike at the root..." the root cause of a dispute being the unmet needs of each person. In the rush of daily living, we do settle for quick fixes all too often. If you ignore the root and rush forward with the excuse that you have more important matters to attend to, then that buried root will spring up and over time shoot forth even more problems.

A root left unattended could strangle you!

Here is a question that will begin the process of digging down to unearth your needs. What would you do if you were <u>guaranteed success?</u> In other words, whatever you decide to do, you would achieve the results that you only dare to dream about!!

What would you do?

By delving into our deepest desires and needs, certain truths and values emerge. I have asked this question countless times, and the vast majority of answers tie in directly with relationship issues. The desire to travel or buy a new house always comes second. Above all else, people long for good relationships.

What would you do if you were guaranteed

success?

Whatever your answer to the above question may be, turn it into a goal statement. I opened this chapter saying if you don't know what you want, there's a very good chance you'll never get it! So take an inventory of your needs. Dig deeply! After you discover your unmet needs, a goal statement will surface. Life is a precious gift! Let's honor each other's needs.

And
now
for a
break.

A Fresh New Voice

We are children of all ages. I'm almost a teenager. Yet it doesn't really matter how old a person is, everyone can feel like

THERE IS NO JUSTICE IN THIS WORLD.

I feel deeply hurt when I am not given an opportunity to tell my side of the story when a conflict occurs. I want to describe what happened during March Break when my mother registered me at a local day camp.

One day I was in the playground and a girl left a swing to do something else, so I took that swing. When she saw that I was swinging, she came back and told me that I must get off. She went on to say that she was going to stop me from swinging. I didn't feel too frustrated because I knew that she could not stop me. This swing was in a public park and I had fair access to it. In the back of my mind, I hoped to get to know this girl, Meg. There weren't too many girls my age, so if I was going to enjoy this camp more, it would be nice to have a friend, someone to eat lunch with.

Meg began yelling at me, demanding that I give her back the swing. The camp counselor came over to ask what was going on. Meg kept yelling that I had taken her swing from her. Then, clear out of the blue, the counselor told me to give her the swing. I had to. **I didn't even have a chance to say what had really happened!!!** I couldn't believe that the loud-mouthed, pushy girl got her way with the counselor. There were other children around who could have told him what they had witnessed. I was thinking, I'm willing to give this swing to anyone but her.

There was no justice. The following poem "The Nap Taker", written by Shel Silverstein, expresses how I sometimes feel:

> "I did not take that nap," I cried,
> "I give my solemn vow,
> And if I took it by mistake
> I do not have it now."
> "Oh, fiddle fudge," cried out the judge
> "Your record seems quite sour.
> Last night I see you <u>stole</u> a kiss,
> Last week you <u>took</u> a shower."[12]

Parents, teachers, and even your best friend can act like a judge by not letting you explain what happened and how you feel. Some people emphasize the bad things, including some made-up bad things, because they want you to feel awful and then they hope you will give in to what they want.

Meg was a bully and when the counselor let her have her way, he actually helped her to become a more powerful bully. She will probably scream louder and longer in order to win the next fight. I can picture her physically pushing and hitting people. Maybe my counselor also believed that might makes right.

If the conflict over the swing had been settled fairly, I may have gained a new friend. Instead I just resented her. That's the sad part, because there are no kids on my street to play with.

My mom and I solve conflicts in an informal way using the mediation process and I'm also involved with peer mediation at school. So I know from personal experience that it's the better way. Fighting just builds up more anger. It's very hard for a child to make an adult stop yelling so her voice can be heard. Please give a child a chance to be heard without interruption.

By Carmen J. Vagiste

Back to the author

Speaking as her mother, I was surprised to read about Carmen's distrust in judges. That may be the result of my exercising her ability to resolve conflicts through the collaborative mediation process. Adults who believe in 'the fight' as a way of dealing with conflicts, tend to run off to a judge with their lawyer acting as their hired gun.

Some people will go to any length to win a battle, in or out of court. They represent the adult version of Meg, the bully Carmen encountered in the playground. The vast majority of legal cases do not need to go to court, but some cases are ripe for a courtroom trial, like the Rosa Parks case.[13]

Children are miniature versions of adults. They are able to talk about their conflicts once their fighting instinct has cooled down. I have visited grade one classes to discuss alternate ways of solving conflicts and am very impressed by the innate intelligence of six year old students. They value being respected just as much as anyone else. We tend to belittle the *silly little fights* kids have and just yell at them, in order to bring it all to an end quickly. In doing so, we're demonstrating the belief that might makes right. And the kids who are yelled at are getting the message, *loud and clear,* that it's okay to control people by yelling. Thus, at the very next opportunity, the same fight gets replayed more noisily than before!

I felt the deep hurt that Carmen experienced when she lost the swing that was rightfully hers. Her loss was as significant as the loss of work is to an adult, whose job was grabbed by a loud mouthed, pushy person who blabbed some mistruth about him. What a child does during the day has as much value as what an adult does. Yet we usually attach more importance to an activity that has a dollar value connected to it. It's deeply ingrained within us.

Treating other people, be they old or young, with respect and kindness gives them a clear signal that we value them. The worst crime is one that never gets reported. It occurs countless times every day. A child is powerless in the face of adult verbal and physical abuse. In receiving the abuse, that child is also receiving training in how to abuse others. A child's brain is like a sponge in that it absorbs everything, without filtering out the mean, vulgar actions.

We honor a young person, each time we sit down to listen to their perspective of a dispute. If we collaborate with young people in the resolution of conflicts, they will begin to see that justice exists in their little corner of the world. A child learns the first human rights lessons at home. The standards that guide us are learned at a very early age. In fact, they become relatively unchangeable and operate in subtle but compelling ways that are often beneath our conscious awareness.

Dr. Goleman writes the following passage in, *Emotional Intelligence*; "Perhaps the most disturbing single piece of data in this book comes from a massive survey of parents and teachers and shows a worldwide trend for the present generation of children to be more troubled emotionally than the last: more lonely and depressed, more angry and unruly, more nervous and prone to worry, more impulsive and aggressive."[14]

The home is a basic unit of society, and a nation can only become as strong as the moral fiber that is woven into the hearts of the young. Show you value them by encouraging them to think on their own two feet as they struggle to resolve the conflicts in their lives using The Action Plan, which is described next. On page 122 there is a simplified Action Plan for children under the age of twelve. Let their voices count!

Conflicts don't have to be viewed as bad experiences, because something good can emerge from the conflict resolution process. If we fight less, there will be more time for love. The quality of our living reflects the depth of our loving in all areas of our life.

Chapter

Six

Conflict will become a catalyst for positive change when you move it through The Action Plan.

Karin Vagiste

The Action Plan

Do you hear that distant drum roll? The big moment has arrived! You are about to read the detailed version of The Action Plan and realize that you can go through with it!! It isn't that difficult! And the really big bonus is that after you have gone through The Plan once, you will not view conflicts in quite the same way again. Thus mediation can be viewed as a life-changing process. I like to call it the life-affirming process.

If you hire a mediator, there may be a pre-mediation meeting during which you will receive an Agreement to Mediate contract to sign. It states the terms of mediation and outlines the fee payment schedule. If there is no such meeting, you'll be faxed this Agreement, which you sign and return along with an outline of the dispute and your desired outcomes. For a description of Toronto's Mandatory Mediation Program, please refer to Appendix A.

Some people seek guidance on how to best define their goal statement, so I provide them with Personal Profile sheets. Others discuss their legal rights with a lawyer ahead of time. Completing both activities is an excellent idea.

You are free to bring anyone or any material evidence

that will help you to tell your side of the story in a convincing manner at the mediation meeting. For example, if some workmen damaged your wall, having two letters that quote how much it would cost to repair the damage establishes legitimacy to your case. Photographs, maps, letters, medical bills and tape recordings are the most common examples of material evidence.

THE ACTION PLAN

What follows is your six step *action plan*! This interest-based mediation process is broken down into sections that lead to the final resolution. If you have decided on DO-IT-YOURSELF MEDIATION, then I recommend Mediation Teamwork as described on page 132. Whatever the mediator is described as doing will be done by you and the other person who is involved in the dispute. Just follow the straightforward 'script' that is basically comprised of questions that will guide your discussion. The questions were written for a mediator, thus some of them need to be rephrased slightly so they will make sense to the other person. A caucus is valid if two or more parties on one side of the dispute wish to meet privately.

STEP ONE

OBJECTIVE: To promote a positive problem-solving atmosphere by seeking agreement to the ground rules.

The mediator will welcome everyone and then briefly explain his role. Whatever notes are written by the mediator will be disposed of after the meeting. Notes simply help to keep the sequence of some critical facts in order.

The **ground rules** help to ensure that civilized behavior is maintained. There is to be no character defamation. No one, except the mediator, is permitted to interrupt another person who is talking. If young people are present, we state that put-downs and blaming aren't allowed. Everything you hear must be kept confidential. All the information that is relevant to the case must be brought forward honestly. The mediator checks that the people who have the authority to settle the dispute are present.

There is an introduction to caucus, which is an optional meeting usually between you and the mediator in a separate room. A caucus may be called for a number of reasons. A mediator may meet privately with each party as part of a strategy building exercise. Parties on one side of the dispute may need to caucus in order to review the strengths and weaknesses of their case. If a lawyer is in attendance, then she may ask to caucus with her client.

STEP TWO

OBJECTIVE: To arrive at a clear understanding of the conflict.

A common practice is to ask if anyone would like to go first and describe the conflict from their point of view. The facts and feelings of both sides will be expressed eventually. The mediator then paraphrases the key issues, and asks other questions in order to formulate a clear picture of the dispute. Any material evidence is brought forward during this step.

Before moving on, the mediator will ask if there is anything else that either party would like to add. There is no need to feel pressure to move on to the next step quickly, because two or three hours have been set aside to enable you to give complete responses to all the questions.

Here are some sample information-seeking questions:

1) Can you tell us what happened?
2) Do you have any material evidence?
3) How did you feel when.......?
4) Can you describe what really bothers you?
5) Why does it bother you?

If someone has trouble expressing emotion, then suggest that they repeat this sentence as a guideline. Whenever you do
_____ (an action is described), it
makes me want to _____.

STEP THREE

OBJECTIVE: To define the interests, needs and goals of each party. To explore where interests overlap in order to create common ground.

The mediator will first ask questions to determine the interests, needs and goals. Later, areas of common ground will be established.

Sample questions about needs:

1) What would you like to see in the outcome?
2) What are your needs?
3) What interest might lie behind your need for _____?

Sample questions on goals:

4) What is your overall goal?
5) What is most important to you in this case?
6) Why is _____ important to you?
7) What do you value about _____?
    The answer to the above question might lead to a discovery
    that you both share some common values.

Possible caucus questions:

8) What do you think the other person needs to understand
    about you that he or she doesn't know yet?
9) What concerns you most about this case?
10) What might happen if you don't reach an agreement?
11) a) What were you hoping or expecting would happen?
    b) Can you tell me what caused you to expect that?

The interests, needs and goals for each party may be written on a
blackboard or flipchart. If the dispute involves more than four
people, it helps to use a different colored marker for each side.

The following questions will investigate the possibility of shared
interests:

12) Do each of you have an interest in preserving the relationship
    to some degree?
13) What opportunities lie ahead for shared cooperation?
14) How could each party benefit from future cooperation?

Within every single dispute there is *some* common ground. The
mediator will explore possible areas of common interest further,
by delving into **minor interests**.

Some goals may contain similar ambitions which spring from
common interests, or values. A review of interests (major and
minor), will occur and the parties are invited to add any other

relevant thoughts. The mediator analyzes the issues and points out the areas of common ground.

STEP FOUR

OBJECTIVE: To brainstorm for solutions.

First the parties face the challenge of coming up with solutions for their shared interests or problems that emerged from the common ground. Then we move on to address individual needs.

The solutions that are put forward now are not to be judged in any way. Every idea that is offered is accepted, and a list of possibilities is written down. It is very important that these solutions are not even discussed at this stage. The goal is to make the list of solutions as long as possible.

Sample brainstorming questions:

1)   What solutions can you come up with that would meet the needs and interests that were expressed in the last step?
2)   What might you do differently in the future to prevent this type of conflict from occurring?
3)   What would be the most inventive, unexpected solution that you can come up with?
4)   A Brain Teaser: Create solutions that certain professional groups might offer; soccer players, dentists, ministers, etc.

Before moving on to the next step, the mediator will review the entire list one more time. When it appears that both parties have created as many solutions as they possibly could, then the mediator may challenge them further with the following creative exercise. The objective is to dream boldly of unusual, off-the-wall types of solutions. Even though an idea may appear worthless or silly, you never know what it could trigger, or better yet, inspire in the other person. Profound thoughts have been known to originate from an imagination that has been granted total freedom. Some people find it easier if their eyes are closed while some relaxing music plays. Feel free to have some fun!

Laughter would certainly clear the air of any tension. Laughter also helps to reduce the distance between people. As a result, the two disputants may feel a bit like allies, collaborating toward a mutual agreement The list of all possible solutions, half-baked thoughts and jokes is reviewed one last time.

STEP FIVE

OBJECTIVE: To arrive at a mutually satisfying solution.

We begin the process of narrowing down the number of solutions through careful evaluation. Check marks are placed next to the solutions that are favored by the parties. The following questions are designed to encourage reflection, so that the reasoning behind a solution can be better understood.

Sample exploratory questions:

1)   What causes you to think that she should _____?
     (Whatever that particular solution happens to be.)
2)   How did you arrive at this solution?

If it appears that one party doesn't like a particular solution, she will be asked to explain why.

3)   Is there any solution that is unacceptable? Why?
4)   Which solutions make you feel good? Why?

A mediator will challenge the reasoning behind some solutions that appear unjust.

Sample challenging questions:

5) How does your solution address the other party's need for
   _____? (Whatever that need may be.)
6) How is your need for _____ reflected in your
   expectation that he should _____?

In the first blank of #6, the mediator describes the person's need.
The second blank would be filled with a description of something
that prevents that particular need from being met.

7) What's the worst possible result?
8) What's the best possible result?

If one party is unwilling to accept a reasonable solution, the
mediator will seek to understand why by asking:

9) When you say you can't do _____ (whatever action is
   implied by a solution), I'm curious,... what do you think
   would happen if you did?

One dispute has a number of issues feeding it, so now is the very
last chance to clear the air of any remaining trouble spots. A
caucus may be called if the mediator senses that one party is
uncomfortable or anxious. The mediator will caucus with that
person first, and then the other party, even though there may not
be an obvious need for it. In this manner, both parties are treated
equally by the mediator.

Once a solution is arrived at, the mediator (or a lawyer) will write
down all the terms that have been agreed upon and then read out
the memorandum of agreement. The parties move on to answer
the final important questions.

Closing test questions:

10) Do you believe this solution is fair?
11) Is it realistic?
12) How easily can the solution be carried out? Can anyone foresee any possible problems in following the solution?
13) Approximately how long do you think it will take to carry out all the terms of this agreement?

If some adjustments have to be made to the agreement, the mediator will read the revised terms and ask whether both parties are able to make a commitment to follow it. If they are, then the meeting moves on to the final step.

STEP SIX

OBJECTIVE: To print and sign the agreement.

The agreement or contract that is printed must identify the parties by their full names. Include phone numbers and complete addresses. Keep the wording specific. For example, don't say "the refund will be paid as soon as possible." Be precise and state the exact date on which this refund will be paid. Describe exactly how the money is to be transferred – money order or certified check? Name the location where this transaction is to occur. Leave nothing to chance.

In case the issue of enforceability is very important, then you must include the following clause at the bottom of the contract: "The parties understand and accept the terms stated above and intend this agreement to be a legal contract binding upon them and enforceable by a court of law." Such a clause is quite popular, because it allows the contract to be enforced by a judge.

If the parties do decide to build in this extra safeguard in order to protect themselves, then the contract must be written in the form of a legal contract. The five basic requirements for legal contracts are as follows:

1) Each party signing the contract must be eighteen years of age or older. There should be no question of mental impairment, which limits the understanding of the agreement.

2) One person or company must not be viewed as having been taken advantage of in an unfair manner. That would be morally and legally reprehensible. The agreement must not call for any party to commit an illegal act.

3) The wording of the agreement must be definite and specific. For example a contract that states: "Fix the leaking ceiling," is too vague to be enforced by a legal contract. You need to state exactly where the ceiling leak is located, how and when and by whom it is to be fixed, and that you require a guarantee of workmanship.

4) A singular promise by one person to do something does not constitute a contract. A legal contract is to reflect an exchange of services and money, for example, "Person A will pay Person B $500. Person B will rewire the building," or reciprocal promises; "Person A will not let his band rehearse after 10:30 p.m. Person B will call person A about the noise disturbance first before calling the police."

5) Both parties must understand and agree to all the terms of their agreement. A signature of the parties at the bottom of the contract will be satisfactory evidence of understanding and agreement.

Since this book has been written for an international market, I would suggest that you show the contract to your local lawyer to double check its legality and legal soundness. I have, at minimum, covered the basic North American legal requirements. If your dispute involves enormous amounts of money or property, you may feel better if a lawyer reviews your contract to make sure that all rights have been protected. The following clause makes your signature conditional upon your lawyer's review: "The terms of this contract will go into effect fourteen business days after signing, unless a lawyer for either party notifies the Mediator in writing regarding objections."

A final word about the appearance of the contract. Try to word the contract in such a way that it reflects the commitment of both parties in a balanced manner – even if more action is required by one party than the other. A simple way of doing this is to alternate the names at the beginning of each line. For example:

1)   Party A agrees to pay $15,000.00 as full repayment of ____ .
2)   Party B agrees to accept $15,000.00 as full repayment of etc.

If a mediator has been hired, a contract might include the agreed upon dates on which follow-up meetings will occur in order to ensure that all terms of the contract are being honored.

All parties receive a copy of the signed agreement. One copy is locked away in the mediation office. It is highly confidential information. Make a photocopy of your agreement for your own records. The mediator closes the meeting by congratulating the parties on their new agreement.

Now your conflict has become a catalyst for positive change!!

In the vast majority of cases, mediation contracts are honored. This is not surprising, because a person's heart and soul has been written into the spirit of this contract. As I've stated before, if you own the problem, then only you and the other person can work out the best possible solution. Mediation provides you with the opportunity to put forward all the issues that are important to you. Thus your final settlement is customized to reflect the needs that exist on both sides of the dispute. No court proceeding could ever offer you such a meaningful document. Personal ownership of your resolution is a highly valued accomplishment. It is the number one reason why such contracts are adhered to.

It is always wise to know what steps to take, just in case your contract isn't being complied with. First, ask questions to understand what prevented the terms of the agreement from being followed. Then, depending on the answers that you receive, there are two options to consider. You may choose to either rework the agreement or go to court. The cost and time typically involved in setting up and preparing for a formal court date, usually makes even the most stubborn and disagreeable disputants opt for another mediation. At that time, the terms of the agreement will be reexamined and rewritten, so that the parties will be able to adhere to them.

A MEDIATED CONTRACT IS THE BEST WAY TO PROTECT YOUR INTERESTS, NO MATTER WHAT HAPPENS!!

If a trip to the courthouse is being planned, your mediated contract puts you far ahead in terms of achieving the results you want. All the details of your contract have already been worked out by you and the other party. The judge will simply take your contract and move it through a court of law. Rules of Evidence exist in court which legally prevent you from bringing forward information that you think is important and relevant to the resolution of your dispute. Thus the only way to get all the critical ideas across to a judge is to hand him your mediated contract. Your hard work in writing up your own contract has not been lost! For that reason alone, it is never a mistake to go for mediation. So if you haven't written out your goal statement yet, then, shut your door and begin the process.

No one else would dedicate the time necessary to make sure that ALL YOUR NEEDS have been defined in the goal statement. Frankly, no one else cares about the outcome of your dispute as much as you do! Many people live lives of quiet desperation because they don't really know what it is that they want, so how could they possibly help anyone else?

The Action Plan provides you with the opportunity of protecting your important needs. The fact that courts can't be counted on to give fair trials that lead to acceptable decisions, bears repeating. Yet the court's verdict will hang over your head for a long, long time. Courts are infamous for taking power away from good, innocent people.

In *Law's Violence*, Cover writes, "Constitutional law is fundamentally connected to war. Legal interpretation occurs on a battlefield; it is part of the battle." [15] It is due to law's inherent nature of being violent that one side achieves victory. Cover goes on to describe a judge as sitting on top of the pyramid of violence.

From a mediator's perspective, there are times when a judge can be useful in greasing a squeaky wheel. To be specific, when one person clings to unrealistic expectations of what the opposing party should pay or do, a judge can provide a reality check via an early neutral evaluation of the dispute. This evaluation process is very simple. Both parties appear before a mutually respected judge, or senior lawyer, and present their case. The judge will then respond with a non-binding opinion of what would realistically happen if their case went to court. This process has also been used to break an impasse on difficult points that have occurred in mediation.

The judge's input moderates one party's outrageous demands, and thus allows the mediation to roll forward more smoothly. Today you can 'rent-a-judge' to provide non-binding arbitration, which is similar to an early neutral evaluation. A judge hears the arguments from each side and then delivers a non-binding judgment which favors one party.

Such win/lose practices that are connected to a court room

trial are prohibited during a mediation meeting. In order to maintain a spirit of collaboration, the traditional responsibilities of a lawyer, namely: discovery work, objecting to evidence, leading a witness through a testimony, and cross-examining, don't occur before or during a mediation.

When you enter your mediation meeting, listen with your eyes, speak from your heart and think through the process by answering the questions listed in the preceding steps. And most important of all, know your comprehensive goal statement.

A SIMPLIFIED ACTION PLAN
(Suitable for children)

1. Both people agree to these ground rules:
   - No interrupting
   - No blaming
   - No name calling

2. The first person begins telling his or her side of what happening, beginning the sentence with, "I feel upset when..."

3. The second person repeats what they heard, in order to make sure they understand the situation.

4. Steps 2 and 3 are repeated with the other person explaining what happened and the listener repeating what was said.

5. Both people talk about what they need and what solution would satisfy their needs.

6. Both people agree on a resolution.

Chapter

Seven

Concern means realizing what the
conflict is and calmly taking steps
to solve it. Worrying means going
round in maddening, futile circles.

Dale Carnegie

Your Invitation

You have the power to mediate, no matter who your opposing party may be: a nightmare client, a controlling lover, an obstinate teenager, a vindictive boss, or an overbearing insurance agent. Up to this point, I have provided you with the knowledge of the mediation process. Now I will propel you forward to invite the other person to the mediation table.

I hope you have already deactivated your Emotional Spin Cycle, if so, then there's not much left to do but activate The Action Plan! It's exciting to stand on the verge of bringing about a significant change in your life. There's no need to do it alone; just take the first step. By teaming up with your opposing party, you will have double the strength to move the dispute forward from being 'stuck' to 'resolved'.

This chapter will introduce you to some inventive ways of extending your personal invitation to mediation. Every dispute situation is different, so the following suggestions are given only to stimulate your thinking about what you could say. As a last resort, you do have the option of contacting a mediation firm and asking them to extend the invitation on your behalf.

A long time ago, someone said to me that the worst things in life are not the bad words that are exchanged; the worst things in life are the good things that don't get said. I'll never forget the simple truth in that thought. Mediation promotes those 'good things'!

The last time you talked to your opposing party there probably was a fair degree of frustration, if not outright volatile anger. Thus, the first thing you might express in your approach is some regret or surprise at how you lost control. An apology might be appropriate, as long as it's sincere. You might explain that you have now had some time to cool off, and you would like another chance to really understand their point of view. Describe how you were preoccupied with only one side of the story the last time, so you weren't a very good listener. Share a couple of thoughts about the qualities that you value about the other person (everyone has some), and tie that right in with your confidence in his ability to collaborate. A little compliment here will go a long way toward opening the door to mediation! Express how hopeful you are about reaching a satisfying solution by collaborating together. Assure him that the solution both of you work out together, will be far better than anything either of you could dream up by yourselves.

A PERSONAL INVITATION

Before we get to a sample script of what might be said during the approach, I'd like to underline the importance of delivering this invitation in person. A telephone call will not leave the same impression, especially since the last time the two of you talked, emotions ran high; perhaps one of you even walked out on the other. If you phone, you could be providing the other person with the opportunity of hanging up on you.

It would be ideal if you knew where this person always picked up his morning coffee, then you could arrange to be there at the same time and let it look like an 'accidental' meeting. Co-workers and secretaries might be able to provide you with helpful information if you'd like to know about his favorite lunchtime restaurant or club after work. Be innovative! Find out where he walks his dog or plays golf.

If the dispute involves a family member with whom you live, then be alert and catch her when she is in a good mood. Extend an invitation to go for a walk in a casual manner, and explain that there's something special (or sensitive) that you would like to talk about away from the other family members. If you get a distrustful look and a refusal, then say that you have good news and it's important to pass it on privately. During your walk show some enthusiasm when you introduce The Action Plan as being the good news. Explain that you don't like living with the tension that has built up between the two of you. Describe how mediation diffuses tension because it takes the focus off blame and releases anger in a healthy way. We all want that, don't we? Even if the other person is silent, you will have connected with her yearning for a less stressful life.

WHAT TO PACK

You will need one huge sack full of patience and goodwill. You have my permission to photocopy The Action Plan starting on page 110. If the other person has shown a great deal of anger or resentment, it might be a good idea to also photocopy the list of secondary emotions that feed into anger (page 89). It'll be a real eye-opener, especially after you give a testimony about how it helped to understand your own anger.

You're the best judge of when the most appropriate time would be for passing along this information. Be careful not to overwhelm someone by passing along too much information all at once. Take your cue from them; listen with your eyes! How do they react to your first offer of The Action Plan?

Pack along your calendar so that you can reserve a minimum of three hours. You may only need two hours, but imagine your frustration at the end of two hours when you're just around the corner from a really good solution, and the other guy must leave because you had said two hours would do. The following scripts describe three sample openings.

"Hi, do you have a minute? I just want you to know how badly I felt at the end of our last meeting [or conversation]. I wasn't having a good day. Sorry about getting sidetracked like that. With your help, I'd like to sort it all out. When are you free?"

"Jon, our disagreement has been on my mind. I'm sorry about losing control when we began talking about 'XYZ'. I'd like to clear up this mess and I need your input."

"I've had some time to think it over [or cool off], and I came to invite you to resolve our conflict using a brand new approach. I really want to hear your entire side of the story. So how about sitting down to talk it through next Wednesday? I promise not to interrupt this time." (The last sentence is spoken with a smile)

Pause to see if the other person wants to say anything. Give him time to respond; count to ten silently if you have difficulty remaining silent. When an objection is raised, acknowledge it. That objection is very real for the other person, so it's important that you don't start arguing about it. Simply accept this objection and ask if he has anything else on his mind. Make him feel important and valued. He will then sense the sincerity of your invitation to sit and talk things out. Let's move to the second strategy for getting a yes answer to your invitation. It is based on considering the other person's self-interests.

SELF-INTERESTS

A person's words and actions reflect his self-interests. Think back to what has been said in the past. What have other people said about this person? Has this person been consistent in holding a certain point of view? If so, then figure out which interests support that point of view. Double check with a work associate or a friend to make sure that you've interpreted his interests accurately.

BEFORE DELIVERY

Before you deliver the invitation, begin to think from the other person's point of view as you answer these two questions:

1) Why would he say NO to your invitation?
2) What would cause him to say YES?

It is possible to make some fairly accurate predictions. At the very least, you'll be more accurate than the weatherman!! A good prediction will enable you to sidestep major trouble. If there's a risk that this person will say no to your invitation, then clearly spell out that you intend to talk about how his self-interests (describe one or two) could be served by working out a solution together. Laying a valued self-interest right out on the table is a bit like seducing someone with his favorite dessert.

If you don't feel confident in your ability to describe the other person's self-interests accurately, then be honest about that. Here are some ideas:

"Would you please tell me what you're interested in? I'm sure there's a way for us to talk things through so that your interests are addressed. Solving our conflict is very important to me because over the years, I've come to value your input."

"Correct me if I'm wrong, but I think you'd like to see _____ (describe an interest) happen. I'd like to learn more about that. (If you get a cold glare, add the following) There may be something I could do to help."

"I'd like to explore your interest in _____. And I know this may sound strange, especially after our last argument, but now that I've had a chance to think things over, I realize that I share some of your interests. We really need to talk!"

Develop a healthy disrespect for your ego.... temporarily!

Most likely, both of you have played a part in prolonging this conflict, so be open about your contributing role. Humble yourself and shoulder some of the blame. It's a necessary icebreaker when the other person's guard is up. A slight exaggeration of why you're partly to blame, may be in order. In criticizing yourself, there's a good chance the other person will also express some guilt over his own behavior. Achieving a solid solution will be worth every little bit of discomfort you may feel at this preliminary stage!

Expect the unexpected! On the day that you deliver the invitation, the other person may have had to cancel a meeting, and consequently is interested in mediating right away! Thus be prepared with your personal goal statement, and a copy of this book. The questions in chapter six form a script that you can can read out to each other. It's your blueprint for action!

Instead of a warm reception, the person may become intent on drawing you into the old argument again. If that happens, listen calmly. Center your body weight, because when you are physically balanced it is easier to take a slow deep breath to maintain your self-control. Your invitation to mediation has caught him by surprise. He hasn't been able to work through his anger, so he'll probably vent it on you. Allow him to do so, up to a certain point. Here are two possible reactions:

"I have done some thinking about that too, and I can understand why you're saying that. I'm sorry but I don't have the time to discuss it now. Why don't we pick a time and place where we can both sit down to talk?"

"I hear you. I don't feel good about this situation either. I'm here because I value your insights and I believe that if you and I tried to honestly work things out with cool, clear heads, then we could come up with a great solution. A solution that would be much better than one either of us could dream up on our own. What do you say?"

If you're talking to a business associate, there's a very good chance that he's troubled about how slowly this work project is moving forward due to the ongoing dispute. Share your optimism about still being able to meet certain target dates once the dispute has been resolved.

Find out what the other person has heard about mediation and how he feels about it. If he's had a bad experience with mediation, then point out that there are both good and bad professionals, just like in any other field. Introduce the idea of DO-IT-YOURSELF MEDIATION. If he's receptive, show him a copy of the mediation process beginning with the comic summary (page 15). Humor appeals to *some* people; you be the judge of how appropriate comics would be in this case.

If you or someone you know, has already resolved a conflict with mediation, then give a strong, positive report about that experience. Emphasize the great features of mediation.

BEST OF ALL THERE WILL BE
NO surprises
NO hidden agenda
NO devious angles

The mediation steps are clearly written out. The two of you will have a chance to preview all the questions. Before he walks away with the mediation steps in hand, express your appreciation for his willingness to read them. Describe how this same mediation process will prove useful in solving *all kinds of conflicts*. After a couple of days, talk to him again and find out what he thinks about the process. Open the door to the two choices that always exist, DO-IT-YOURSELF or third party mediation (where you hire a mediator). If the other person wants to pursue the former, point out that you hope it doesn't look as if you'll be in charge of the upcoming mediation. Explain that this method of solving conflicts relies on collaboration. So go on to.......

SUGGEST MEDIATION TEAMWORK

Explain how each of you could take turns leading the discussions through the six steps of the process. Volunteer to lead steps one, three and five. Offer him the easier steps: two, four and six. You could pass along a compliment, by joking about the fact that if someone like you can do it you're sure he will find it a breeze. If the other person isn't interested in sharing the steps, then invite them to co-mediate with you.

THE CO-MEDIATION CHALLENGE

Use a bit of humor by describing the two of you as partners in crime, so it's only fitting that you now operate as a proactive pair. As the co-mediator, all the other person does is follow your example and read some of the relevant questions that are listed at the end of steps two to five. You would handle the other mediation responsibilities. If you're able to encourage his active participation in the process, then there's a much greater chance for a successful outcome. In the event that the other person says he has no time to read the sheets, then ask when he could clear some free time. If you are told that such 'homework' is of no interest, then thank him for his honesty. Express your appreciation over his willingness to try something new. When the mediation meeting begins, hand him a copy of The Action Plan, so he can follow along. You will be pleasantly surprised at how involved the other person becomes in carrying mediation forward.

WHEN & WHERE?

Ask for suggestions on where the two of you could meet. Be sure that the location suggested is free from external interruptions, such as people walking in and phones ringing.

"I'd like to meet at your convenience, so that we can solve our differences together. Most mediations take about three hours. Please tell me when and where you would like to meet?"

If you are talking to someone who flatly refuses, try appealing to his sense of adventure.

"I thought you enjoyed trying something new at least once! Remember the time you _____[describe a specific example]. This is similar, so (with a twinkle in your eye), isn't it time for another risky venture?"

Most people, no matter what their age, are willing to try something new at least once. Let him know that after he has experienced mediation that is truly collaborative, it will change how he is going to deal with other conflicts that come up in his life. There is absolutely no harm done by sounding like a blind and bleeding optimist. The other person will feel complimented by your faith in their ability to learn and adapt to something new.

CUSTOMIZE Your Invitation

Your very first few words have the power to lead to a mediation meeting, or crush your hopes of ever achieving a satisfying solution. You can't afford to be lazy when a personal or professional relationship might be lost or rebuilt to last. There are no shortcuts! As you write out the dialogue for your customized invitation, keep in mind the other person's self-interests, and try to predict their response to your words.

After the words are down on paper, it's time for a few rehearsals. A great deal is at stake when you offer your invitation, thus it can be a nerve-wracking, brain-numbing, heart-thumping, or hand-sweating ordeal!! For a successful invitation, you have to at least *appear* relaxed and confident. If you rehearse your lines well, you will be able to carry through, no matter how nervous you might feel on the inside. When preparing for an audition, actors memorize their lines, then take deep breaths and long, slow stretches to calm their nerves before showtime. Memorization certainly isn't required here. A quick review of the Sixty Second Break on page 65 will be helpful. It'll prepare you to overcome any negativity. This time you will steer clear of slipping into the Emotional Spin Cycle if your Hot Button gets pushed.

REHEARSAL TIPS

HOW you say something is more important than WHAT you say. Studies by Dr. Albert Mehrabian at the University of California, Los Angeles, show the various levels of importance a conversation has to a listener: words, 7 percent; the sound of the voice, 38 percent; and the visual, which includes facial expression, body language and clothes, accounts for 55 percent of your total impact. It is difficult to evaluate the quality of our voice as we're speaking, so audio tape your invitation. The connections we make in life are fragile; why leave anything to chance?

When you play back the invitation script that you've recorded, you have another wonderful opportunity for visualization. Those who practice this deceptively simple method of visualization will exude confidence. First move away from external noises and assume a relaxed body position. Press the play back button and then close your eyes and visualize that other person for whom the invitation has been customized. He or she is standing right in front of you. Fill in the details; what is she wearing, how is her hair combed, where is she standing? Do you see the warm expression on her face? That person is already nodding yes to your invitation, before you've finished listening to your last few words! Don't underestimate the power of visualization.

A HEROIC ACT

What is a heroic act? Trophies are handed out to people who rescue others from burning buildings and other calamities. Helping others is often easier than helping oneself to overcome some personal difficulty. Some people would rather run out and save the whole world, than rescue themselves from a painful and messy dispute.

A heroic act involves sitting down with your 'enemy', looking them straight in the eye and helping them to understand the benefits of mediation. That first step you take when you deliver your invitation to mediation could lead you to experiencing one of life's rare, golden moments. Your courageous actions of

COLLABORATING with the 'enemy' instead of
CONQUERING the 'enemy' deserve a badge of honor.

Create a memory that you can proudly pass on to your children and grandchildren. You will have distinguished yourself by turning against the tide. A successful mediation experience is more exciting than winning a fight. After a fight, you have to always be on the lookout, for you never know when a counterattack will sneak up on you.

It's common for friends, family and coworkers to expect you to fight it out because that's how it has *always* been done. Dare to initiate the unexpected. In most organizations, schools and churches, it's incredible how people mirror each other, from their dress code to how they think, and even the jokes that they will let themselves politely smile at! There is a great deal of pressure to conform.

BREAK OUT OF YOUR BOX!

There's too much mediocrity in this world. When you decide to step out of your comfort zone, select a simple dispute for your first mediation experience. Many peace-making opportunities exist all around us.

If your very first DO-IT-YOURSELF MEDIATION doesn't succeed, that's okay. Even seasoned professionals don't succeed every time. What we do in that case is call it a 'no deal' and reschedule the meeting for another day. I provide specific questions for my clients to work out before the next mediation. Some people need to sleep on the issues in order to clear their minds, so they can open up to other possibilities A relaxed, fresh mind is able to be far more creative the next time around.

If the mediation stalls a second or third time, there's no need to quit. Hire a trained mediator. You'll zip through the initial steps of the mediation process in no time and then have the mediator lead you through the difficult part. The desire to rise above our disputes, whether large or small, is common to all of us. View your invitation as a peace offering that represents the key to freedom. Once that dispute has been resolved, you'll be set free from the stress that zapped your mental, emotional and physical energies.

FREEDOM

People work very hard to gain freedom from stress, which has become a modern-day affliction. Jogging, biking, swimming, weight lifting, playing tennis and a multitude of other sports help to promote some relaxation. A good workout releases endorphins, which make us feel fine for at least a couple of hours. The very next day, if not sooner, when we meet up with whatever caused our stress in the first place, nothing has changed. The same old conflict stresses us just as much as before.

No matter how much your sweat glands pour as they relieve you of muscular tension, the source of your mental stress remains locked in. The Action Plan provides a shake-out for the mental tension that has built up, because it removes the root cause of your conflict. This kind of change provides enduring freedom. The agreement that you sign sets you off in a new direction, so that you won't have to return to that same stressful scene.

The bird is a popular symbol of freedom. One legend describes how the Canadian Native Indians feel the pulse of the eagle's blood in their veins. They have a saying that within every eagle there dwells the spirit of freedom, and within every person there dwells the spirit of the great bird. Go ahead and connect with a person's yearning for freedom when you invite her to mediate. Inspire her to soar to great new heights!

Many Happy Mediations!

Endnotes

1. Carter-Scott, Cherie, *If Life Is A Game, These Are The Rules,* (New York: Bantam-Dell-Doubleday, 1998), p. 21.

2. Robbins, Anthony, *Awaken The Giant Within,* (New York: Simon & Schuster, 1991), p. 129.

3. Gelinas, Paul, *Coping With Anger,* (New York: Rosen Publishing Group, 1988), p. 84.

4. Williams, Redford, *Anger Kills,* (New York: Times Books, 1993), p. 107.

5. Carnegie, Dale, *How To Stop Worrying and Start Living,* (New York: Simon & Schuster, 1984), p. 116.

6. Goleman, Daniel, *Emotional Intelligence,* (New York: Bantam Books, 1995), p. 62.

7. Lovenheim, Peter, *Mediate, Don't Litigate,* (New York: McGraw-Hill,1989), p. 6.

8. Stiebel, David, *When Talking Makes Things Worse,* (Whitehall & Norton, 1997), p. 53.

9. Lovenheim, Peter, *Mediate, Don't Litigate,* (New York: McGraw- Hill, 1989), p. 4.

10. The needs that were listed on page 85 were general in nature, and thus could easily tie in with business disputes as well. The following needs are more directly linked with business issues.

    NEEDS
    - To project a solid business reputation
    - To maintain membership in a professional association
    - To repair a sales relationship
    - To be forgiven
    - To promote fair business practices

11. The nonblaming communication model is equally useful in the home environment. In our home we hung it on the washroom mirror using a small metal hanger which is attached to a suction cup. You can also tape a magnet to this communication model and post it on your fridge. If it is visible, *it will be used.*

12. Silverstein, Shel, *Falling Up,* (New York: Harper Collins, 1996), p. 140.

13. In 1955, Rosa Parks broke the law when she refused to take a seat at the back of the bus because she was black. By going to court she set an important legal precedent – after her trial the law was changed to allow black people to sit anywhere on the bus.

14. Goleman, Daniel, *Emotional Intelligence,* (New York: Bantam Books, 1995), p. xiii.

15. Sarat, Austin and Kearns, Thomas, *Law's Violence,* (Ann Arbor: University of Michigan Press, 1992), p. 228.

Appendix A

Mandatory Mediation in Toronto

In June 1997, the Attorney General sent the Civil Rules Committee a proposed rule for the mandatory mediation of certain proceedings in the Ontario Court (General Division). After numerous meetings, an extensive consultation program, and many amendments, it was approved by the Civil Rules Committee as Rule 24.1 (Mandatory Mediation). Rule 24.1 provides for a mandatory mediation session in case managed actions.

Under the Rule, local mediation committees are established and mediation coordinators are designated to administer the program. The Rule does not effect undefended actions. In a defended action, after the filing of the first defense (that is, after the filing of the first notice of intent to defend, statement of defense, or notice of motion in response to an action,) the parties will have 90 days to carry out a mediation session.

Within 30 days after filing of the first defense, the plaintiff is obliged to file with the mediation coordinator a notice stating the mediator's name and the date of the mediation session. The parties may select the mediator from a list of mediators compiled by the local mediation committee or they may select a mediator from off the list. In either event, the mediator must comply with the mandatory mediation rule.

If the mediation coordinator does not, within the prescribed time, receive the notice stating the date of the mediation session, an order abridging or extending the time for the mediation session, a consent postponing the session for up to 60 days, or a notice that the action has been settled, then the mediation coordinator will assign a mediator from the list compiled by the local mediation committee. The assigned mediator shall immediately fix a date for the mediation session and shall, at least, 20 days before that date serve on every party a notice stating the place, date and time of the session and advising that attendance is obligatory.

At least 7 days before the mediation session, every party shall prepare a statement of issues and provide a copy to every other party and the mediator, and the plaintiff shall provide the mediator with a copy of the pleadings. The parties, and their lawyers, if they are represented, are required to attend the mediation session, unless the court orders otherwise. All communications at a mediation session and the mediator's notes and records shall be deemed to be without prejudice settlement discussions.

Within 10 days after the mediation is concluded, the mediator shall give the mediation coordinator and the parties a report on the mediation. If there is an agreement that settles the action, it shall be signed by the parties or their lawyers, and the defendant shall file a notice of the settlement, in the case of an unconditional agreement within 10 days after the agreement is signed and in the case of a conditional agreement within 10 days after the condition is satisfied.

Perell, Paul M., *MANDATORY MEDIATION: The New Rule – How will it really work? Chapter one, 1-13 to 1-15.* The Law Society of Upper Canada, Department of Continuing Legal Education 1998

Order Form

If you would like an extra copy for someone else, a classroom set, or whatever your needs may be then, order by phone from Canada & US: (800) 565-9523 or (416) 667-7791 or fax the order form to:(800) 221-9985 or (416) 667-7832.
One copy costs $10.95 in the US and elsewhere, $14.95 in Canada
An order for 10 or more books will receive a 10% discount.

Mail me _____ copies of SETTLE IT! (0-9682157-1-8)	$_____
Deduct 10% discount if relevant	_____
$4 Shipping charge for 1 book (US. & Canada)	_____
(add $1.00 for each additional book)	_____
Overseas: $5.00 for the first book	_____
(add $2.00 for each additional book)	_____
Canadian orders add 7% GST for books & shipping	_____
New York State orders, add 8% sales tax	_____
TOTAL AMOUNT	**$_____**

Payment: ☐ Enclosed is my cheque/money order,
           Payable to: University of Toronto Press for $_____
           Mail to: University of Toronto Press, Order Department, 5201 Dufferin Street, North York, Ontario, M3H 5T8, Canada
      ☐ Please charge my: ☐ Visa   ☐ Mastercard

Card #_____ Expiry date_____

Signature (required)_____
Name:_____
Institution:_____
Address:_____
_____
Phone: (_____)_____

The author as speaker

Vagiste is a warm, dynamic speaker who welcomes speaking invitations to a variety of professional organizations, associations, schools, parent groups, and churches. She holds a deep commitment to teaching and helping people to settle their conflicts. She also holds a couple of degrees: University of Toronto, Education; York University, Communications; and a Mediation Specialization, Windsor University, Faculty of Law.

If you are planning a conference and would like to consider her as a keynote speaker, or a seminar leader, then please photocopy the form below. Be sure to include a description of your event, its location and an estimate of the number of people who may attend. Please attach your business card. Thanks.

Name: _____

Organization: _____

Address: _____

_____

Telephone: ( ) _____

E-mail: _____

Mail to: Solid Solutions
28 Sommerset Way, Suite 1015
Toronto, Ontario, M2N 6W7 Canada
E-mail: kvagiste@freenet.toronto.on.ca

Thank-you for your interest.